TRIBES

a process for social development and cooperative learning

by Jeanne Gibbs

CENTER SOURCE PUBLICATIONS • SANTA ROSA. CALIFORNIA

Library of Congress Cataloging in Publication Data
Gibbs, Jeanne.
Tribes: A Process for Social Development and Cooperative Learning

"A new revised version of Tribes: A Process for Peer Involvement, first published in 1978 by Center Source Publications."

Includes index.
1. Learning, psychology of.   2. Social Learning.   3. Self-respect.
4. Classroom environment--United States   5. Academic achievement
I. Gibbs, Jeanne. Tribes: A Process for Peer Involvement.   II. Title.

LB1084.G52   1987   370.15'23   86-72796
ISBN 0-932762-08-5

Printed in the United States of America

Additional copies of this book may be ordered from
Center Source Publications, 305 Tesconi Circle,
Santa Rosa, California 95401.

This book was designed and illustrated by Sherrin Bennett
Printed by Publisher's Press

CONTENTS

Acknowledgements

How did this book evolve? It began many years ago as I watched my own young children struggle as strangers each time we moved to a new school in a new town. It began with my own search for close friends and caring community. It began with an ever-growing awareness that the values of individualism and competition may have blessed our Western world with amazing achievements accomplished by the strong, but left behind was a wake of "losers" engulfed in failure, alienation, delinquency, alcohol/drug abuse, unemployment, despair, lost dreams and hopelessness. Massive funding to remedy problems of the lost still fails to stem the tide. It is rare that dollars and energy are dedicated towards preventing problems rather than treating them. Moreover, it verges on being heretical to suggest that a different approach needs to be taken by all the caretaking systems...schools, families, daycare programs, youth organizations and human service agencies themselves. The thought began to percolate some sixteen years ago: What if those systems altered their own environments so that people learned to live alternative values, such as: cooperation, altruism, respect for individual differences, kindness and love? Would all then have a better chance to grow to their fullest innate potentials?

Encouraged by other explorers, my purpose became one of finding answers to those two questions. This book represents a synthesis of social change and human development theory to assist educators touching the lives of children to build supportive learning environments. The ecological approach evolved out of the pioneering work of Urie Bronfenbrenner and Kurt Lewin. The developmental theories of John Dewey, Benjamin Bloom, Margaret Mead, and Piaget all contributed to imagining a better way of "calling forth" the best in people. During more recent years, the concepts on which we based the Tribes process have been validated by the behavioral and educational studies of people like Elliot Aronson, Laurel Tanner, Robert Slavin, David Hawkins, Lee Robins, Cheryl Perry, David and Roger Johnson.

There are so many creative people along the way who have used the Tribes process for a wide variety of programs such as, social development pre-schools, peer support groups, the prevention of delinquency and substance abuse, social support in residential facilities, interactive conferences, school climate improvement, staff management, youth leadership, health promotion and community empowerment models. Now hundreds of teachers are using Tribes as a process which can integrate a wide range of cooperative learning methods. My wish is that all of the innovators and explorers could indeed be credited by name. The network of Tribes continues to grow. More than anything we have been and always will be a cooperative learning community... sharing ideas, processing what works and doesn't work, and redefining "a new way of being together." We are glad that now YOU have picked up this book. Welcome!

Welcome to Tribes!

Sausalito, California   *Jeanne Gibbs*

1

THE TRIBES STORY

1
The Tribes Story

For a long time concerned teachers, parents, counselors and school administrators had been groping for effective ways to motivate children's learning, bring up test scores, manage classroom behavior problems and perhaps have people (including the teachers) enjoy schools more. National studies and surveys were alerting the general public and even rattling the U.S. Congress that public education somehow was not adequately preparing students for the complexities of today's world. Among the alarming symptoms of the educational system's failure were:

- a decline in national academic test scores;
- an increase in school drop-out rates, student behavior problems, delinquency, teenage pregnancies, suicides, and the incidence of alcohol and drug use; and
- an increase in the numbers of teachers complaining about "burn-out" or simply choosing to leave the profession.

Assessing the Situation

Way back in the fall of 1974 some educational consultants at the Center for Human Development in California began to look at the whole picture in a different way. They were a group that liked to make great long lists on large newsheets and analyze data (you know the type!). The first lists they made were very depressing because they listed all the deficiencies typically observed in many children:

- low self-esteem
- anti-social behaviors: lying, teasing, and fighting
- disrespect of teachers
- lack of motivation
- apathy, depression and alienation.

Then they listed all that many teachers, administrators and parents were saying. Parents were alarmed that many youngsters could not read well. School board members were becoming more concerned that achievement scores were edging downward each year. Teachers were saying that no matter how well they pushed through the curriculum, the quality of student

work seemed to be declining. And administrators who live in that no-man's land between the parent community and faculty were becoming aware that switching from one program to another each year was not bringing up the scores. (The same concerns may still be felt at your school!)

A suggested solution came from some parents: "Let's go back to the basics . . . back to the basic three R's of reading, 'riting, 'rithmetic. Just drill the kids, give them more homework and get up the test scores." It was then that we decided to consult a friendly computer named ERIC (Educational Research Information Clearinghouse). Out of the printouts on research studies came a bit of enlightenment:

SEARCH: CORRELATES TO INDIVIDUAL ACADEMIC ACHIEVEMENT & PROBLEM BEHAVIORS

69-1082   Direct correlations of self-esteem to reading scores.

71-0381   Correlation of low self-image to achievement and behavior problems.

23-1588   Anti-social behavior in young children predicts early use of alcohol and/or drugs.

12-8923   External locus of control in adolescents correlates to juvenile delinquency.

92-4701   Direct correlation: teachers & peers negative perceptions of academic ability to arithmetic achievement.

The work of Dr. Benjamin S. Bloom, Distinguished Professor, University of Chicago (theoretician of "Bloom's system of taxonomy" for learning subject matter), states that by the time a student has completed secondary school he/she has spent 20,000 hours in school; **and** he has experienced **two curricula**: the "manifest" one in reading, writing, arithmetic etc. and the "latent" curriculum of social interactions. Bloom questions which of the two curricula will be of more lasting imprint . . . the facts of the history lesson or . . .

- the humility of being an isolate,
- the fear of being teased,
- the confusion of feelings unexpressed,
- a feeling of powerlessness when pressured by peers,
- the ways that decisions are made and rules enforced,
- the partiality of a teacher towards other students.

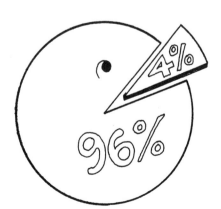

Bloom estimates that 96% of the 20,000 classroom hours are devoted to the manifest curriculum, and a mere 4% to time to address the latent curriculum.[1] And we wonder why Johnny can't read!

Positive Clues

The real "zinger" came one day when a computer search turned up some **positives** that hardly anyone in school systems at that time was talking about!

65-1133	POSITIVE PEER REGARD IMPROVES SELF-IMAGE!
76-4501	COOPERATIVE PEER TEACHING-LEARNING METHODS LEAD TO HIGHER TEST SCORES!
31-0788	A POSITIVE CLASSROOM CLIMATE EN-HANCES MOTIVATION AND IMPROVES BEHAVIOR!

Now none of these three positives had anything to do with identifying, working, treating or doing remedial work with "deficiencies" in individual children. They had to do with **peer relationships**, **teaching methods and the environment of the classroom.**

Social Environment and Human Behavior

The realization that environment conditions behavior is still largely ignored by educators, physicians, therapists, and human service personnel plugging away in traditional fashion to teach, treat, serve or shape up children. We call the individual deficiency approach the "repair shop methodology." It begins with a diagnosis that you have something wrong with your carburetor (a deficiency). Immediate solution: go to an expert who will "fix it," and when you or your carburetor look shiny again, back you can go to the mainstream of folks who are still thumping along O.K. This method of simply identifying the poor readers, the "problem kids," and often those considered developmentally disabled simply overlooks the impact negative environment may be making. Some forty years ago a behavioral scientist, Kurt Lewin, published work stating that:

"Human behavior is the product of the interaction between the growing human organism and its environment."[2]

As obvious as this sounds, the "systems approach" to dealing with human behavior and learning is still considered radical even in this age which credits systems theory as the reason we were able to get to the moon some decades ago.

What is School Climate?

The climate of the school or classroom is the atmosphere or feeling that pervades it daily. It is the music underlying the words . . . an energy that either contributes to or detracts from children's social development and opportunity to learn. A positive climate evolves out of . . .

- an atmosphere of trust
- a sense of belonging and community
- involvement in decision-making
- kindness and encouragement from peers
- teacher's energy and morale
- the teacher's authenticity, non-judgmental attitude, fairness, and congruent communication to students
- clear expectations, goals, learning outcomes
- classroom and school practices concerning cooperation rather than competition

Dr. Urie Bronfenbrenner, Professor of Psychology and of Human Development and Family Studies, Cornell University, defines **human development** (which should, we believe, be the goal of all educational systems!) as:

> "the person's evolving conception of the ecological environment and his relation to it, as well as the person's growing capacity to discover, sustain or alter its properties."[3]

We concluded that students in schools everywhere need to be supported daily by a climate which:

1. challenges their social development in ever-widening diverse groups of people and settings throughout their school years;
2. gives them the time and practice to consciously reflect on their surroundings;
3. helps them internalize the social skills and the capacity to manage, and improve the settings that surround them;
4. motivates interest in learning and personal development;
5. enhances self-esteem so that they may achieve academically and feel empowered to live life well.

"But," said a startled teacher, "to convince teachers and schools to change from their traditional ways will take a lot of doing. Few of us understand how social development correlates to behavior and learning. Many simply write off any consideration of the affective development of children as time consuming and irrelevant to education. Teachers will have to be convinced of a pay-off not only for the children but themselves. We'll have to have training to know how to intentionally create that magic **classroom climate** you folks talk about."

Defining the Basics

Today's world is not the one of twenty-five years ago. Concerns for peace rather than war, cooperation rather than competition, kindness rather than cruelty, social justice rather than discrimination, team management rather than dictatorial leadership and our entry into a high tech informational age call for different skills and consciousness.

The skills are **relational** and consider the human condition. They are based on some old fashioned democratic values such as **respect for individual differences whether cultural, racial, religious or unique life-styles.** As parents and educators we are challenged to think through the too often neglected American values of altruism, kindness, cooperation and consideration for all people in our pluralistic society. A fine new study calls these essential but less practiced human values "habits of the heart."[4]

If we are again to incorporate these basics in educational settings, it means setting new goals for the personal development of **all** individuals and their capacity to effect systemic change. It means working from a multi-cultural perspective not only **to include** the disempowered (minorities, the handicapped and any who feel limited opportunities) but to develop the capacity of critical thinking in all young people so they are empowered to assess and improve conditions around them.

One can only conclude that long before the academic basics can be taught to children, there is a fundamental set of "3R's" that begin at birth. They are the true "basics," the habits of the heart so desperately needed in today's world. We believe that RELATEDNESS, RESPECT AND RESPONSIBILITY are the true basics. Remarkably enough, children who master these pro-social skills and attitudes feel better about themselves and others. They have a sense of self-esteem. And self-esteem not only correlates to positive behavior but to greater achievement in the academic basics of "Reading, Riting and Rithmethic."

Social Development

The relational "basics" may be considered the corner-stones of each child's social development. If indeed, we believe as Urie Bronfenbrenner does that human development is the person's growing capacity to discover, sustain or alter his ever-evolving environment and his relation to it . . . parents and educators must better understand the stages of social development. We must **intentionally** create environments and activities that support each student's respective age level of development so that an ever-expanding consciousness of self, others, world and universe evolves.

Our goal should be to prepare and empower our children to interact competently with the people and systems central to their journeys in life. Those who are not well prepared, whose social development is arrested, become the casualties of society. They are the ones who see themselves as misfits, disenfranchised or powerless. It is well known that the quality of interactions with the many sociocultural variables in each child's life more accurately predict deviant behavior than either psychological or demographic variables.[5] An example of this are the studies clearly showing that young children who exhibit anti-social behaviors (lying, stealing, hurting peers etc.) are most likely to become involved in early drug use.[6]

We are indebted to the work of Gerard Egan which emphasizes working with the individual in the context of the systems or environment that surrounds him. The illustration which follows shows the ever-widening complex with which each person must learn to interact well.[7]

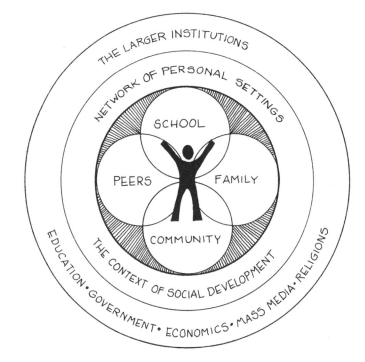

Social development means acquiring the basic relational skills, positive self-esteem and a sense of value and responsibility in a widening world. Just as the life of all growing things is based on the concept of expansion, social development leads the individual beyond a focus on "me" to the wider perspective of "we," our society and world.

By becoming aware of the particular stages of social development that our children may be in at any one period of time we can encourage and support their respective stages of personal development. The two-page chart which follows summarizes both the cognitive and social development stages of children from two to seventeen years old. The key systems which impact their development, are shown as well as implications for school programs. Since the Tribes program is used extensively as a model to prevent the use and abuse of alcohol and drugs, the chart references some program implications for that purpose.

Unfortunately, most of us as teachers may have been trained only in the "cognitive stages of development," and consider social development as adaptation to outer-controls. We assume that the child who sits quietly,

THE STAGES OF COGNITIVE AND SOCIAL DEVELOPMENT IN CHILDREN AND YOUTH

AGE/GRADE	KEY SYSTEMS	COGNITIVE DEVELOPMENT	SOCIAL DEVELOPMENT	PROGRAM IMPLICATIONS
2–4 Preschool	Family	**Preoperative Stage** ● magical thinking ● circularity ● difficulty dealing with more than 1 or 2 causes ● confuses physical-psychological causes of illness ● developing language skills	● emphasis on self ● oriented to parents ● needs limits, secure environment ● developing motor skills	● build self-esteem ● support social development (sharing, taking turns, asking questions) ● provide safe caring environment
5–7 Kindergarten to 1st Grade	Family School Neighborhood	**Preoperative Stage** ● magical thinking ● circularity ● difficulty dealing with more than 1 or 2 causes ● confuses physical-psychological causes of illness ● concrete mental operations	● emphasis on self ● identifies with own gender ● enjoys group play ● oriented to parents	● build self-esteem ● support social development ● involve parents in activities & knowledge social stages ● encourage sharing, caring behavior ● use cooperative learning groups
7–11 2nd to 5th Grade	Family School Neighborhood Peers	**Concrete Operations** ● begins to think relationally and to generalize ● becomes capable of integrating several variables in causal relationships	● oriented to parents ● enjoys group play & peer relationships same gender ● often competitive or has difficulties with peers ● often unaware of behavior affect on others ● impressed by older role models ● learns behavior from parent/peer role models ● more concerned about physical image than social ● may begin using drugs	● train parents & teachers in prevention ● use small groups (social skills) ● use cooperative learning groups ● provide feedback on behavior ● use curriculum on licit drugs & decision making ● provide non-drug using groups & activities

THE STAGES OF COGNITIVE AND SOCIAL DEVELOPMENT IN CHILDREN AND YOUTH
(continued)

AGE/GRADE	KEY SYSTEMS	COGNITIVE DEVELOPMENT	SOCIAL DEVELOPMENT	PROGRAM IMPLICATIONS
12–16 6th to 10th Grade	Family Peer Group School	**Normal mental operations** • capable cognitive problem solving • things abstractly & hypothetically • integrates multiple factors to understand concepts	• oriented to present rather than future • preoccupied with self presentation, acceptance by peer group, physical maturity • seeks initial sexual intimacy • seeks peer role models • motivated by social effects of drug use • seeks independence in decision making • differentiates between self and environment • feels awkward in social skills • experimenting and using drugs	• provide life skills curriculum & peer role models teaching refusal skills • use cooperative learning methods • encourage responsible decision making • promote peer leadership, peer counseling programs • involve in improving social environment • use role model peers to teach drug curriculum
16–18 11th to 12th Grade	Peer Group School Work Family Community	**Relativistic thinking:** • capable of synthesizing wide range relational material	• primary concern: individual identity, financial independence, deepening relationships, self-exploration, distancing from family & making own decisions • concerned more with psychological effects drugs than social or physical • oriented to peers	• empower leadership • involve in business ventures community projects and drug-free alternative activities • implement curricula focused on health, social economic and legal consequences of misuse alcohol and drugs

politely raises his hand, gives back answers and never causes commotion is doing well. Yet this child may not be able to make friends, communicate well, take an independent stand in the midst of peers, negotiate with others, or feel empowered to alter negative conditions in life. He may be manipulative, secretive, lack self-esteem and the capacity to be self-responsible. **Indeed, social development is neither compliance nor adaptation to conditions imposed by others.** It is a sequential set of relational skills, attitudes and competencies which also are the foundation of each child's self-esteem.

Self-Esteem . . .
The Key to Life

The primary resource predicting the success or failure of each person as a human being is a precious energy known as "self-esteem." The adolescents who still demonstrate stages of social development appropriate only for very young children are arrested in their growth. Indeed, they are stuck at earlier infantile stages and become problems for parents, teachers, peers, society . . . and themselves. Sensing their inadequacy, they live self-confirming prophecies that "I am not capable . . . I cannot learn . . . I am no good at anything." They lack positive self-esteem.

One educator sums it up this way. "Deep inside there is a longing . . . a hollowness wanting to be filled. It is a need to **connect** with a positive sense of self and with others. The more positive the self-image, the less painful the longing . . . the less positive the self-image the more painful the longing. Too often we use temporary "fillers" such as drugs, alcohol, compulsive anti-social activities to blot out the hunger and give a **temporary sense of self.** It is only as we find positive self respect and "connectedness to others" that we can sense our true value. The painful longing diminishes and the hollowness is filled with self-worth. It is then that we even self-confirm positive images of ourselves."[8]

Studies have shown that self-esteem is not related to family, education, wealth, social class, geographical living area, father's occupation or having mother at home. It comes from the **quality of relationships that exist between the child and those who play a significant role in his life.**[9] It is a **person's assessment of "the self-pictures" reflected back to him from others daily.**

Self-esteem is "a quiet inner knowing saying I'm glad to be me."[10] It is a sense of self-respect, a feeling of self-worth. Three main areas convey loveability and worth to children:

- affirmation of their positive qualities from parents, teachers and other significant caretakers;
- affirmation from peers and siblings;
- affirmation to themselves based on their own experiences of competency or success ("I did that well." "I am good at reading." "Arithmetic is easy for me.")

> Children value themselves to the degree that they have been valued.

To focus upon academic achievement without focusing on building self-esteem and social development is putting the cart before the horse. Exhaustive research documents the correlations of positive self-esteem to achievement in reading, arithmethic and other subject matter. No well-meaning teacher can do it alone. Not only must parents understand their important role, but methods for peers to affirm each other must be introduced into all educational settings.

Learning is a Social Phenomenon

If we look into most classrooms in America today we would recognize that educational methodology is **teacher-centered**. The teacher stands in front of the class, has set the goals, spends the day asking virtually all the questions, calls on students to answer, responds to their answers, points out concepts, draws conclusions, and somehow maintains discipline. For the most part, students sit quietly until called upon. Restlessness, disruptive behavior and sometimes caustic remarks signal boredom. The traditional approach ignores the fact that we are **social** creatures stimulated by social interaction (which, of course, is held to a minimum in classrooms). Contrary to what we may want to believe, learning in not a passive activity dependent upon teachers pouring ideas and facts into small heads. Real learning is an exciting generative process that happens between those who want to learn . . . it is a social phenomenon which cannot simply be teacher-centered.

Social interaction and learning happens in groups of people. Research on the effectiveness of having children work in small learning groups has fostered countless new reading programs and awakened educators throughout the country to **cooperative learning** methods. Group-centered learning focuses the group's attention on the task it must complete rather than the teacher standing in front of the classroom. It is the group's responsibility to achieve learning outcomes. It is the teacher's responsibility to be a consultant, a guide, a facilitator . . . to intervene only when necessary. Shifting from traditional teacher-centered structure to group centered learning is not easy without training, sound theory and the development of the teacher's own group skills.

WHAT WOULD HAPPEN IF

. . . all schools and classrooms had a way to develop positive environments for social development and learning?

. . . each child in every classroom felt supported by peers who helped to strengthen each other's self esteem?

. . . teachers had a way to have students become responsible for themselves and each other?

. . . parents recognized the importance of social development to their child's academic achievement, and decided to help build the **3 R's of Relatedness, Respect, and Responsibility** in the home?

Our Hope for Danny

In our mobile society, thousands of young people are moving into new schools and classrooms daily. Imagine for a moment a small friend of ours named Danny. He is insecure, shy, and has moved about so much with his family that he is labeled a "poor learner." If Danny is finally lucky enough to come to a school which has the Tribe program, he will immediately become a welcomed member of a supportive peer group. For the first time he will not struggle to make friends. Peers will convey their acceptance of his unique background, values and talents. They will become his classroom family. Working cooperatively on subject matter they will celebrate his progress in their learning group.

For the first time Danny does not have to struggle for inclusion, and perhaps act out to gain attention and influence in the new community. As he develops a sense of trust with his tribe he becomes comfortable in asserting his own individuality. Repeated experiences of respect from peers enables him later in the teen years to take a stand in the midst of a negatively-oriented group and say "I am not going to smoke pot with you guys or cut class today." He has learned refusal skills and to be responsible for his own behavior.

As Danny's tribe works cooperatively on curriculum they become responsible **to each other** for completing tasks. The teacher gives them time to reflect on how their group gets along, who is in leadership, and ways to improve the quality of the group's time together. The teacher transfers the responsibility to Danny and his tribe for problem solving many behavior issues.

The big "plus" is that Danny's teacher no longer has to do it all herself, but counts on four or five classroom tribes to make her teaching more effective. The teacher becomes an expert facilitator of small groups that assure the supportive environment for social development and academic achievement. She finally has a system that relies upon positive peer power rather than a battery of outer controls which she has generated.

What Really Happened?

Our fantasy became a proposal which received funding from the Department of Education, State of California. Now that was more than 10 years ago. We conducted a pilot in one elementary school and by the end of that school year celebrated the fact that twenty-six teachers working in their own "faculty tribes" had proven the model was effective in:

- improving self-esteem,
- enhancing respect for teachers,
- lessening behavior problems, and
- motivating elementary children to learn subject matter.

Equally important, the teachers reported that for the first time they felt better about themselves and enjoyed more positive support from other teachers.

The years in between that pilot program and today have brought many refinements to the Tribes program. Evaluations throughout many schools continue to verify the program's effectiveness with a wide range of populations. Of particular interest is the success with **special education** children, both the developmentally disabled and those with learning disabilities. Schools having diverse **ethnic** populations have realized an increased acceptance of individual and cultural differences.

We realize now that the Tribes program was ahead of its time. More than anything it has been a forerunner of the now popular cooperative education movement. Current research on **cooperative education** confirms our own observations that:

- students achieve more in cooperative interaction then in competitive or individualistic interaction;
- students are more positive about school, subject areas, and teachers when they are structured to work cooperatively;
- students are more positive about each other when they learn cooperatively than when they learn alone, working competitively or individualistically (regardless of differences in ability, ethnic background, handicapped or not);
- students are more effective interpersonally; are most positive about taking part in controversy and have better developed interaction skills.[11]

Our biggest surprise is that the Tribes program (which is more of a process that a set program) is applicable to the needs of many populations and systems. Not only has it changed the environments of schools but also of juvenile facilities, pre-schools, after-school daycare, recovery homes, recreation centers, residential schools, college classes, board meetings, large conferences, rehabilitation centers, community youth groups and peer counseling programs. We are overwhelmed!

The last chapter of this book has some overviews and sample activities for applications within pre-school/daycare programs, families and staffs. We plan to publish separate books of many of the successful adaptations. The purpose of this book is to provide the theory and "know how" for the use of the Tribes program in educational settings.

> "What is most needed in the schools is not new personnel or equipment but a new philosophy and a new structure for using what we have."
>
> William Glasser, M.D.[12]

2

WHAT TRIBES ARE
AND HOW THEY WORK

2 What Tribes Are and How They Work

I f we were really "telling it like it is," we would call our program something like, "Sociometrically Balanced, Permanent Membership, Positively Oriented Peer Groups for Social Development, Responsible Behavior and Cooperative Learning." Now aren't you glad we call it "Tribes" instead?

You could possibly argue that there are significant differences between our tribes and tribes like the Navajos and Watusis. It's just that so many people began calling these small supportive groups "tribes" . . . because they recognized the similarities of identity, support and community inherent and admired in native tribes. We wanted a term that would symbolize "belongingness" and would set Tribes apart from other group techniques.

A "tribe" is a group of five or six children who work together throughout each day throughout the school year. If possible they are seated together in a circle of desks or at the same table in their classroom. Each classroom, depending upon its size, may have four to five tribes. The activities that the tribes engage in generally fall into three categories:

- sharing personal concerns, feelings, and positive regard for one another;
- planning, problem-solving and maintaining an environment of positive support for all members;
- working cooperatively on curriculum as assigned by the teacher.

The tribes are formed sociometrically to distribute boys and girls, students of high and low peer acceptance and special problem children.
Students have the opportunity to name friends that they would like in their tribes, but it is the teacher who determines who will be in each tribe.

The teacher never participates directly in the groups, but acts as a "facilitator." The teacher gives directions, sets time limits, and maintains control by intervening only when necessary. He/she recognizes that responsibility must be transferred to the students to manage the tribes so that **peer support** enables the achievement of program goals.

The power of the tribes process is realized as positive peer regard begins to improve self-image and behavior. Children depend upon the approval of their friends, and most are much more influenced by a remark from a peer than an adult. This influence is the key to the tribes process: positive peer support for social development and learning.

The Goals of the Tribes Program

1. Children who maintain long-term membership in supportive classroom peer groups will **improve in self-image, behave more responsibly, and increase their academic achievement.**
2. Teachers will spend less time managing student behavior problems and have **more time for creative teaching.**
3. Schools, organized into the tribes system, will create a **positive climate for learning.**
4. Parents will report a carry over of **positive statements and attitudes** from their children into the home environment.

A Tribes school is a community in which teachers, administrators, students and parents all enjoy the mutual respect and caring that is essential for growth and learning.

Positive School Climate . . . A New Way of Being Together

In order to establish a positive environment in the classroom, the Tribes teacher introduces four ground rules that students are to honor at all times when in their small groups. We call these expected behaviors the "norms" of the Tribes Program.

The Tribe Norms

1. **Attentive Listening:** paying close attention to one another's words and feelings; giving another caring respect and consideration.

2. **No Put-Down's/Appreciation:** avoiding negative remarks, name-calling, hurtful gestures and behaviors; instead . . . treating others kindly and stating appreciation for their unique qualities, value and helpful contributions to others.

3. **Right to Pass:** choosing when and to what extent you will participate in group activities; recognizing that each person has the right to control himself though within a group setting.

4. **Confidentiality:** honoring the group's sharing; reminding each other, "No gossip-no names"; being confident that "what we say here . . . stays here."

These important ground rules are posted in a prominent place in the classroom. The teacher asks people to help each other remember the important norms. Through modeling and many activities in the community circle, the new way of being together begins to happen. Whenever smaller groups of students are formed, the teacher reminds all of the rules again and transfers the responsibility to the groups to maintain the positive guidelines. These norms are essential to transforming the classroom into a positive caring learning climate.

Uniqueness of the Tribes Program

There is a veritable bandwagon today of schools moving to cooperative learning methods. Experience and research has finally convinced educators that:

- learning is a social phenomenon and can no longer remain teacher-centered;
- attention must be given to children's social development as well as academic achievement;
- a positive school climate enhances learning; and
- promotion of cooperation rather than competition brings up academic test scores.

Programs such as the Magic Circle, Student Teams-Achievement Divisions, Jigsaw, Teams-Games-Tournament, Cooperative Learning Teams, and Student Team Learning all are oriented to similar goals and methods. Teachers are trained to divide children into various groupings, divide up lesson plans, and assign tasks to be done cooperatively. Too often, however, the small groups begin to have difficulties as they try to work together.

There are fundamental reasons why student learning groups may be less than successful in working on tasks together. Teachers who quite naturally are focused on accomplishing the lesson plan may overlook the need to **first** build a high level of trust both within the classroom and cooperative learning groups. More often than not students are either assigned randomly to groups or are reassigned to new groups too often. Achieving any sense of trust, inclusion or affiliation then becomes extremely difficult. The difference between just using random learning groups and the environmental classroom approach of the Tribes Program looks something like this:

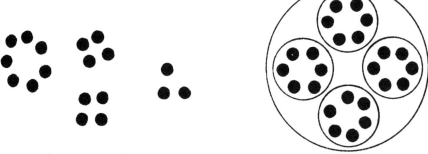

Random Learning Groups   **Tribes Cooperative Classroom**

Random groupings produce a scattered energy with less inclusion and make it more difficult for students to work together. The system of long-term membership in the Tribes process, assures a consistent positive energy within each small group and the entire classroom. Tribes, an **intentionally created support system**, sets the stage for achievement by structuring a positive classroom climate. In summary, the Program is a synthesis of theories and methods which:

- places students in long-term support groups;
- builds inclusion and trust within the groups prior to working on tasks;
- sets aside time to reflect upon individual and group learning experiences;
- uses a proven group development process to create a positive learning environment;
- has a set of protective "norms" (groundrules) that assure a safe positive climate;
- transfers responsibility from the teacher to students to help maintain the learning environment, solve problems, and be accountable for completion of tasks;

- emphasizes teacher and peer role modeling to teach interpersonal skills and caring behaviors;
- focuses on children's social development to enhance academic achievement;
- promotes a respect for and acceptance of individual differences (ethnicity, culture, handicaps and learning disabilities); and
- is recognized as a model program for the prevention of delinquency and substance abuse problems.

TRIBES IS A PROCESS . . . THE MUSIC FOR THE WORDS!

Stages of Group Development— "The Tribes Trail"

There is a curious map on the following page which is one of the main secrets to the magic that happens in the Tribes program. O.K., we hope you think our map looks like a magical journey. It really is our attempt to detail the important synchronization that takes place between the role of the teacher-facilitator and the development of small groups in the classroom. The success of any group's life together and individual achievements of its members depend upon the facilitator's knowledge and ability to orchestrate sequential activities appropriate to the group's particular stage of development. It strikes us as sad that though all living takes place in groups . . . we seldom are taught how to make groups work well together. Families, labor unions, churches, parent-teacher associations, management staffs, faculties and classrooms . . . all in search of positive participation and a reliable democratic process.

"The meeting will come to order. Tonight's agenda was mailed to you. The secretary will read the minutes. The executive committee **has decided** that all members will . . ."

Ignorant of any group development theory, most of our organizations struggle in limbo somewhere between the "great man theory of leadership" and "democratic process" waving Robert's Rules of Order to maintain control. As a member, you may never feel as involved as the leaders are. You may wonder why you are there and how the group will ever really know what you have to offer. YOU, the real special "you" are seldom invited to express your opinion or possible resource to the organization. In time your interest wanes and you drift onward hoping for more recognition or support in some other group.

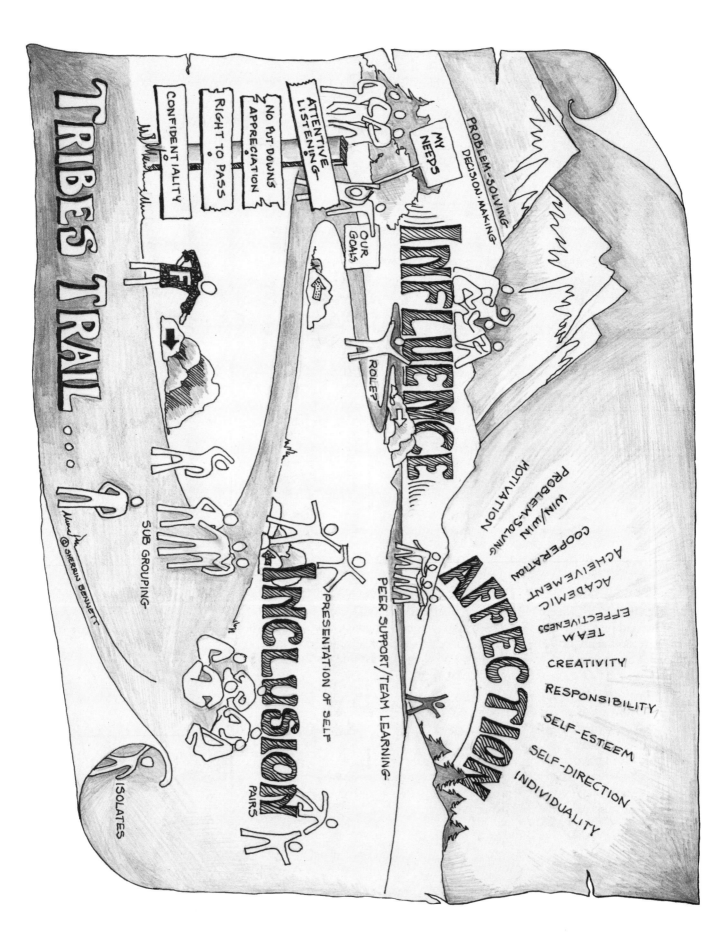

The reason that people become "drop-outs" whether from their families, schools, groups or other relationships is because they do not feel **included** and **of value** to the others. Paid employees (yes, even teachers and administrators) also manage to drop out, but in subtle ways such as: not following through on responsibilities, absenteeism, sabotaging a department's plans, caucusing with other disgruntled peers, manipulating meetings or being apathetic.

This organizational **dis-ease** is a veritable plague in school classrooms. Too many students say they feel unsupported by others, isolated, hardly noticed by the teacher or peers. They question whether they have any value, influence or power in the daily class community and either act out their frustration or become apathetic. Few educators are aware of a basic principle:

> If a person does not feel included, he/she will create his own inclusion by grabbing influence (attracting attention, creating a controversy, demanding power or taking control)

Student behavior problems stem from the need to have attention either from authorities, family or peers. **IF** we can learn ways to help **all students feel included and of value** a major educational and family concern, antisocial behavior problems, will be on its way to being resolved.

All guides taking people into a wilderness need a map so that the community of people traveling together arrive at their hoped-for destination. As a classroom group facilitator, it is essential that you understand some simple stages of group development and the major issues that arise as your students learn to work cooperatively in learning groups. The Tribes Trail Map shows a facilitator and shaded arrows to illustrate a gradual shift in the teacher's role from being directive, providing much structure, to becoming less directive and providing less structure. As the members of your classroom groups develop a sense of inclusion and are ready to take initiative (to be of influence and value), they themselves are encouraged to assume leadership in their groups and the classroom. The net effect of this subtle process is that responsibility is transferred to students themselves. This is why the Tribes process is known as one that "calls forth" the latent talents and resources of any organization's members and enables tasks to be accomplished by all in satisfying and creative ways.

It is this intentional transfer of leadership in the midst of a positive and caring environment that makes the Tribes Program unique from all other cooperative learning methods. It is the "big secret" to building self-esteem and motivation among children. No matter what the age level, it gives a loud and clear message . . . "you are capable people who can indeed manage yourselves and help each other!"

The Stage of Inclusion

Now let's look a bit closer at how this works. Notice on the Tribes Trail Map the separate individuals about to enter the groups, classroom, staff meeting or organization. As mentioned above, the shaded arrows along the path indicate the degree of structuring that the facilitator provides for people as they come from their many separate paths. Each person entering the group is unique in his/her life experience and perceives the new classroom situation out of a personal complex of diverse needs and expectations. All newcomers to any group feel an initial anxiety and have many unspoken questions:

- I wonder if I'll like this classroom?
- Will the teacher and other kids like me?
- How will they get to know me? I feel scared.
- Why am I nervous?
- I wish this were the end of the day not the beginning.

Knowing this, the responsibility of the teacher-facilitator is to live up to the name "facilitator" . . . which means "one who makes it easy." If people stay immersed in these initial anxieties, they cannot learn and in time will demonstrate acting-out behavior. They will find their own "comfort zones" . . . which may not be positive for either themselves or others. A student may simply show restlessness, shuffle papers, get a stomach ache or in time become regarded as one more learning handicap. A teacher who never feels comfortable in her faculty may be inattentive at meetings, irritable with students and simply suffer through to the end of the year.

Three basic opportunities must be provided within all organizations:

1. Each new member needs to be able to **introduce him/herself,** not just be stating a name but offering a short description of his/her feelings, interests, resources, talents or special qualities.

2. Each person needs to be able to **express his/her hopes or expectations for** what will happen during the group's time together (**our agenda!**).

3. Each person needs **to be acknowledged** by the group as having been heard, appreciated and welcomed.

In a classroom it may take several days or weeks for each student to present him/herself either to the total class or within a small group. In organizational settings (like faculty meetings), initial **inclusion** means having adequate recognition and the same opportunity to present oneself prior to tasks and agendas. It means **balancing persons and tasks** and this makes the big difference in how people finally are able to work together.

As soon as possible the facilitator begins to model and teaches the **norms of the Tribes group development process.** To minimize anxiety, make it easier to get acquainted and build inclusion, people are invited to meet in small temporary groupings (pairs or triads). Observe any organization of more than six people. They very naturally sub-group or arrive at a meeting with one or two others in order to feel less anxious. The intentional use of small temporary groups early in a meeting makes it easier for all to feel included at least with a few others before relating to a larger group of people. Leaders of large conferences, using our process, sub-group hundreds of people early in the gathering just to guarantee no one is isolated. In such settings, agenda items can be submitted from all of the small groups in order to include the expectations of all participants.

Inclusion is a basic human need, and unless it is met people feel vulnerable and defensive. The saying "a camel is a horse designed by a committee" most certainly refers to a committee whose members attempted to undertake a task without first having achieved inclusion together. Time spent "up front" building inclusion and trust is the most valuable commitment a group can make. Although it takes a bit longer at first, the pay-off in achievement makes all the difference!

The Stage of Influence

As mellow as the stage of inclusion can be, in time a very natural restlessness signals that people are ready to move on . . . they feel empowered and they are ready to grow! Yet why this sudden restlessness? The Teacher-facilitator begins to notice many new indicators in dynamics of the groups:

- members are taking more initiative; they are making suggestions and questioning/criticizing the current leadership;
- group goals, ways to work together and make decisions are being debated;
- people are not being as polite or as patient with each other;
- conflicts are beginning to arise.

Now rather than panic and decide that "groups just don't work," these indicators are positive signals. The new restlessness means that the time spent in building inclusion, trust, kindness and a sense of belonging has been achieved. People are now ready to really work on tasks together . . . the stage of influence has arrived. Congratulations!

The **influence stage** centers on the questions:

- how can each person influence the goals, tasks and decision-making process of the group?
- how can members assert their individuality and value in the midst of the group? And
- can leadership be shared so that the resource and potential of each member "is called forth"?

To feel "of influence" is to feel of value (worth, power, individual resource to the group). To the extent that each person does not feel important in a classroom or organization, commitment and motivation decrease. Rather than allowing group members to wrestle for ways to have influence, the skilled facilitator provides a selection of activities that help people to:

- express diverse attitudes, opinions, positions and personal feelings;
- put forth ideas without the others passing judgment; help people to respect individual differences;
- use participatory methods for decision-making so that all members feel they are influential and of value to the group;
- help members share leadership responsibility.

The role of the teacher-facilitator is also to suggest appropriate methods for the groups to deal with issues and concerns. Conflicts and misunderstandings are a natural part of the process not to be ignored. They can be openly resolved through a wide variety of strategies such as:

- reflecting on and discussing the incident or situation that is happening;
- helping people to state their feelings clearly;
- assisting the group to give constructive feedback;
- suggesting problem-solving methods;
- role-playing, using role-reversal techniques; and
- negotiating the priorities of individual members.

> **If issues are ignored, the energy of the group is deflected away from its capacity to accomplish tasks together!**

The sensitive classroom teacher recognizes that continuing to focus on subject matter in the midst of interpersonal or group issues is neither academically nor emotionally helpful. Having people meet in their tribes to talk about the disruptive situation and suggest ways to resolve it, not only transfers responsibility to the class for the concern, but promotes a sense of value for the students. Once the conflict has been handled, hopefully using student suggestions, the academic subject may be addressed again with renewed energy.

During the **influence stage** the teacher-facilitator becomes less directive, allowing groups to operate as much as possible on their own. The teacher maintains contact with the groups by requesting periodic reports and circulating among the tribes to determine whether assistance is needed. If the teacher-facilitator were to sit within a group, the dynamic changes immediately with group members again centering on the teacher rather than their involvement with each other. As the influence stage progresses and issues become resolved, shared leadership begins to emerge from individuals in the group. What a delight it is to see the shy child of the class lead an activity in his/her tribe! And what a relief it is to see the dominant member sit back as the others in his/her group assert their unique talents. Some folks have called the process "**magic**" . . . but we call it a real possibility that can be achieved by any committed teacher.

The Stage of Affection

Affection is a vital component of the entire Tribes process from the first moment that the newcomer hears appreciation in the inclusion stage to the satisfaction of group accomplishment during the influence period. On the Tribes Trail Map, you will see that we noted the Affection Stage at the end of the trail even though it hums along throughout all of the process stages.

The fact that from the very beginning there are **no put-downs** and **attentive listening** is assured for people in this process means that warmth and kindness is realized early. The **social support** that children enjoy in a tribal classroom encourages their social development and learning. As **each child** begins to feel proud of his/her own creativity, leadership and self-direction in the midst of the groups, a state of affection just seems to happen.

Often we are asked, "But aren't groups bad for children because they make them conform?" The answer would be "yes" if it were not for the space that the Tribes process allows for the individual at all times. The norms say "you have the right to pass, you will not be put down in this group, people will be listening and caring about you." This guarantees the protective environment that calls forth individuality.

Affection is the result of feelings, ideas and contributions being acknowledged. It is the state of affairs where the tribe members have a basic commitment to care for and support one another. It is the warmth and satisfaction of having worked together well . . . it is the laughter after the storm . . . and the essence of one unique soul meeting another.

The Spiral of Renewal

But you ask, "How about the teacher? There must be a whole batch of teachers sitting around without much to do once those tribes have achieved the three stages of development." It is true that often the successful group facilitator feels as if no one notices him anymore or remembers his efforts once the tribes have become working groups on their own. Not to worry . . . the facilitator is never "put out to pasture," for small groups will always need help to facilitate their continuing tribal evolution.

Each time a tribe meets, it needs some type of inclusion activity before it can work well together, and it will always experience influence issues that need to be resolved. A helpful way of visualizing the continuing growth and evolution of a tribe is to imagine an ascending spiral which moves up through the levels of inclusion, influence, and affection as it rises. One full "loop" represents a group meeting, so that each time the spiral completes a cycle it goes through the three stages again. But each time a tribe meets, though it still needs to begin with inclusion, it moves on to a slightly higher level of positive interaction. The spiral is continuous and a never ending process. Graphically, it looks something like this:

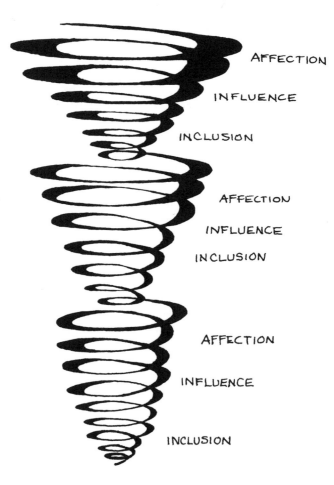

AFFECTION

INFLUENCE

INCLUSION

AFFECTION

INFLUENCE

INCLUSION

AFFECTION

INFLUENCE

INCLUSION

The repeated sequence of inclusion, influence and affection enables the group to experience increasingly more profound interaction the longer they are together.

Although we have been experimenting and evaluating this process for many years, there is still so much to learn. What matters most for us are the reports back from students, teachers, administrators and even parents who say that they emerged a bit more **special in their own self-worth** because they had the opportunity to be part of a "tribe" somewhere. It may take some new effort to integrate the process into educational settings, but the sensitive teacher recognizes the tremendous benefits that can happen for the Dannys of the world. We think this brief poem by a fourth grade tribal teacher says it best:

Burnt out
So what if he can't read
Teach him how to love
Himself?
Me?
Others
Lost in a stack
of paper
That good guy note
he needed
I needed
The look in the eyes
when you finally
dig it out
The eyes say
For me?
from you?
a warm moment
in a cold day
It passes
math time
You forget
They remember. . . .

Joe Rhodes
Antioch Unified School District
Antioch, California

3

THE TRIBAL
COMMUNITY

3
The Tribal Community

I magine for a moment that you have been invited to visit a tribal classroom. Arriving just before class begins, you are greeted by the teacher. As the children enter the classroom you notice that the voices and movement are different from many other classrooms . . . there is no pushing and shoving. You hear no "put-downs." The teacher raises her hand, and one by one as children notice her gesture they stop talking and raise their hands until the entire class is quiet. The teacher greets the class warmly and introduces you. There is a murmur of excitement about the presence of a stranger, but the teacher continues. "How is everyone this morning? Let's all gather in our community circle." The class rearranges itself, sitting in a large circle. Two students urge you also to sit on a small chair in the circle. The teacher raises her hand, and one by one as children notice her gesture they stop talking and raise their hands until the entire class is quiet. "To build our community inclusion this morning, I suggest that we go around the circle and share something good that may have happened for us lately. Be brief so everyone has a turn. Let's listen attentively to each other and remember you have the "right to pass" if you do not care to share this morning. One by one the children begin to speak:

> "My dad played catch with me last night for a real long time."
> "Colin is coming to my house after school today."
> "Our tribe invented a great new game."
> "My puppy isn't sick anymore."
> "I brought some bamboo today for our tribe's project."

A few said they would like to "pass" . . . no one pressured them to participate. Everyone was listening attentively. The teacher nodded or made statements of affirmation; she often thanked people for sharing. Panic! It was your turn. You felt warm inside . . . and said, "I'm just so glad I'm here. I feel a part of your community already."

*   *   *   *

If after reading this little vignette, you don't have any questions, you need read no further. If, on the other hand, you sense the magic and are a teacher who would also like to learn how to **intentionally** create it each day, please stay with us. The material in this chapter will enable you to:

- develop a positive social climate in your classroom before forming small learning groups;
- model and have children learn the "norms" of the Tribes process;
- build **inclusion** for the total classroom community.

Building Community

Before long-term membership tribes are formed, several weeks of inclusion activities are used to "build community" in the total classroom. This period of time permits all of your students to get to know each other, to learn the important norms and to establish a positive social climate. As the day begins, the teacher invites the entire class to sit in a large circle; here the Tribes program is similar to the Magic Circle[13] or Glasser's Classroom Meeting.[14]

In this configuration, it is the teacher who is the leader, directing all the activities. He introduces and models the norms and encourages the students to participate. As soon as the children become familiar with the process of participating in a group sharing activity and understand what behaviors are expected when in a group, the teacher has them meet in temporary small groups. This enables students to experience something of what their longer membership learning groups will be like; and it gives the teacher an opportunity to see how different combinations of children work together.

Among the basic skills that each teacher must learn are those of leading activities appropriate to the group's stage of development, follow-up discussions, and time for students to reflect upon their learnings from the experience.

Leading a Full Group Activity

So there you are with twenty-six faces looking up at you expectantly. Remember the Tribes Trail Map? Yes, here in the beginning it is up to you to be directive . . . to help all become comfortable and feel included with you and one another. Your primary responsibility now is to make it safe for people to share and to convey by word or gesture how glad you are that they are part of the classroom. The quality of the classroom environment is strongly influenced by your personal style, the behavior that you model and expect from your students. **What** is talked about during a community circle session is usually less important than **how** the group interacts together.

Let's say that for this initial full-group experience you have chosen the activity titled "Three Tribles." First, be sure that all people are sitting in a large enough circle so that each person can see all the other faces. Your students will probably chatter among themselves while the circle is being formed. Be patient and observe their interactions. Soon they will settle down and you can get started.

Tell them that this year "our class will be working together in some new ways in small groups so that people can help each other. We will meet often as a whole class talking together in a community circle like this."

Somewhere during this first introduction raise your hand and tell them that this is how you will ask for their attention. It is a non-verbal signal. Whenever people see the teacher's raised hand it means everyone stops talking and also raises their hands. You might state that this means they will never have to hear you shout or screech. Now how many people would like that? (Ask for show of hands.) It is also a great test of our awareness or consciousness. Are the same people the first to notice . . . are the same the last ones to become aware?

Teaching and Modeling the Norms

If it is appropriate for the students in your classroom to enter into a discussion of what they need in order to feel safe or trusting in a group, take the time to do this rather than simply posting the Tribe norms. They can do this as a brainstorm in smaller groupings or as a community circle discussion. Undoubtedly, people will say things like:

> "I need to know I won't get punched or put-down."
> "I want people to listen to me when I talk."
> "I don't want to get pushed around."
> "I want my privacy."
> "I don't want to do something just because everyone else does."
> "I don't want our group to fight and hassle all the time."
> "I want people to like me."

After the brainstorm help the class see similar statements, summarizing them into the basic four tribal norms: No put-downs/appreciation, right-to-pass, attentive listening and confidentiality. Even though you may have a beautiful graphic of the norms ready for posting, save it for the next day or have the class make them after this important discussion. The point is to have your students "own" the new rules as much as possible.

Of course, this initial activity may not be possible with younger children or all populations. In that case, do your graphic ahead of time and have it posted in a prominent place in the classroom. Tell the class that these norms or rules not only help people get along well together and but make people feel good about themselves. It is also possible that some of your class has been introduced to them previously in the school; if so, ask one of those students to explain them. This is a way of encouraging your class to take responsibility for modeling and maintaining these important behaviors.

Your own modeling is absolutely the most essential factor in teaching the new ground rules. Much is written and said about teacher modeling. We have concluded it is not simply making positive statements or giving points to students throughout the day. Simply modeling a technique is not the same as the heart-felt message that comes from your authentic inner-self. One teacher said, "no matter what my voice and eyes are saying, if my heart isn't present, I remain separate from my students." Effective modeling means being **CONGRUENT, REAL, and HEART CONNECTED.** It means:

- setting aside a lesson plan long enough to tune into a student's concern or pain;
- being non-judgmental, patient and caring even to the more difficult ones;
- avoiding at all cost the subtle put-downs in the midst of your frustration or stress;
- standing on your own rights . . . to pass, to state your feelings, to say "no, I choose not to do that. It would not be good for me."
- affirming through warm eye contact or a gentle touch on the shoulder;
- laughing at your own mistakes; conveying your own fallibility and commitment to life-long growth and learning.

It is being there in an authentic way, consciously present of the existential moment . . . touching, speaking and listening with your heart.

Attentive Listening

Attentive listening means that whenever a person is speaking all other people acknowledge the speaker with full attention and eye contact. Others do not interrupt; they respect one person speaking at a time. Attention is paid not only to the **words** but also the **feelings** behind the words. It means that people are not running their own agendas or conversations in their heads though pretending to listen. In some of our bilingual Spanish speaking classrooms, the lovely word "atentamente" seems to say it well.

Listening and communication skills truly need to have a place in school curriculum. They affect children's ability to learn academic material. This is especially important as classrooms move toward **cooperative educational methods.** Some of the listening skills which should be practiced include:[15]

- attending: listening silently with full attention
- non-verbal encouragement (nodding, "Uh huh")
- paraphrasing ("What I heard you say was . . .")
- reflecting feelings ("You sound **angry** . . .")

There are many activities in this book which can be used to teach your students this essential life skill.

No Put-Downs . . . Appreciation

If one of our main objectives is to develop self-esteem in children, school systems and families must find ways to eliminate the scores of derogatory or negative remarks that bombard young people each day. Unfortunately put-down remarks are a basic form of communication among children themselves. At times they are used in families to convey affection: "you good-for-nothing," "you bum," "you crazy character." Though off-hand or flippant, they are hurtful remarks that not only damage self-esteem, but undermine the level of trust felt by members of a group. A positive climate which builds self-esteem cannot develop unless you, the teacher-facilitator:

- challenge students themselves to prohibit the exchange of put-downs (also known as "burns," "cuts," "cold pricklies"), **and**
- encourage students to exchange statements of appreciation and positive regard (strokes, validation, recognition, "warm fuzzies").

Enforcing the "No Put-Downs" norm can be a tedious process in the beginning. You will be tested frequently because students will want to find out if you **really** notice and mean it. If you are consistent, patient and help them to express how such remarks hurt others, before long the children themselves will intervene when they hear any violations.

When confronting a put-down, be careful not to put down the "put-downer." Instead: "Aaron, don't forget our class has agreed not to hurt people by using put-downs."

Even though positive, caring communication is encouraged, this does not mean that negative feelings are not allowed. One way to encourage your class to confront put-down statements and to express negative feelings is to ask the child who was on the receiving end to use an "I-Message" telling the sender what he felt when the put-down occurred. Example: "I feel sad when I'm called 'stupid,' Aaron. That's a put-down and I don't like it!"

This is the beginning of positive peer influence and the assumption of responsibility by the children themselves to maintain a positive classroom climate.

The power of minimizing put-down statements is half of the step towards building student self-esteem. The other secret is to replace the put-downs with statements of positive appreciation. You might want to tell the class that as we quit hurting people with put-downs we will discover that just as a coin has two sides . . . our put-down norm sign has a secret on its other side that will help everyone feel great about him/herself. Helping people of any age to express positive statements to each other is often like going swimming against a strong current. We think it is a sad commentary on our society that we all probably make five times as many negative comments to each other in the course of a day rather than affirming the value of ourselves and those around us.

The chart indicating the stages of social development shows that for children under six parents are key to their young worlds and thus are central to developing positive self-image and a child's sense of value and competency. As children enter the school years, the regard of peers and teachers becomes an essential component of their social development. Thus, the Tribes Program intentionally incorporates statements of appreciation throughout each school day; and it urges schools to help families do the same.

Statements of appreciation are invited after every activity and modeled by the teacher throughout the day. Initial resistance and shyness can be overcome by telling younger children the Fuzzyland Story, by Claude Steiner,[16] discussing its meaning and doing follow-up activities such as:

Fuzzyland Map	Boasters
Warm Fuzzies	Warm Fuzzybag
Sharing A Warm Fuzzy	

In order to help people start making statements of appreciation, it helps to give them some sentence starters such as:

"I liked it when . . . (describe the situation)."
"I felt good when you . . ."
"I admire you for . . . (describe the quality)"

After completing a group activity, write these phrases on the chalk board and ask each child if he/she would like to give someone a "warm fuzzy" or statement of appreciation. Your own modeling encourages the sharing of positive statements perhaps more than anything. It is important that you model being both a good "giver" **and** a "receiver."

Examples:

"I liked it when you shared your dream with us, Dawn."
"Thank you, Josh, for telling me you liked my funny joke."

The Right to Pass

The "Right to Pass" means that each person has the right to choose the extent to which she will share in a group activity. It is the essence of our democratic beliefs not to be coerced, to have a right to one's privacy and to take a stand apart from a majority. Without such a guarantee, individual freedom within a group is not protected. "To pass" does not necessarily mean that one is not participating. Being a silent observer is a form of participation, and often leads to greater learning. The "right to pass" means one prefers not to share personal information, feelings, or actively participate at the moment in the group's activity. It is a choice to remain quiet or to protect oneself. It is a personal right that must be repeatedly affirmed by teachers and peers as "O.K. . . . you have the right to pass. It's just fine to do so."

This protective norm is essential for all groups and organizations. Permission to pass within a group setting gives a necessary sense of control. It encourages students to be self-determined and responsible for their own well-being even among peers. It gives the practice and courage to stand back from situations that either are not comfortable or are contrary to one's own values and well-being. Drug abuse prevention programs for secondary students emphasize the "teaching of refusal skills." The slogan "Just Say No" has become very popular. We are convinced that the teen years are a bit late to begin learning refusal skills. Experiencing that "I have the right to pass . . . to be me, and not to go along with all the others" is essential even for very young children.

Many teachers are anxious that if this norm is used in classrooms, students will pass on learning subject matter. First of all, the norm does not apply when individual accountability is required on learning tasks. Students do not have the right to pass on homework, taking tests, responding to the teacher etc. They do, however, have the right to pass on peer-led activities. It is important to keep in mind that:

- not participating does not mean that one is not experiencing and learning;
- the cooperative learning group itself will in time draw the person who usually passes back into an active working role.

Again, healthy development for young people means that they become inner or self-directed . . . rather than dependent upon outer controls or pressure from others.

Confidentiality

Confidentiality means that "whatever is said here . . . stays here." Like the "right to pass" norm, it protects and honors individual integrity. It does not mean that a student cannot go home and tell her parents about a group activity and what **she said or did** in her tribe. It does mean that she does not have her group members' permission to disclose what someone else may have said. Children need to have the right of confidentiality, but not a right to gossip.

The concept of confidentiality for classroom learning groups may become controversial if you do not clarify this difference. For children it can be remembered simply as: "**No names-no gossip.**"

One way to teach this important norm is to have each tribe make lists of how people feel when someone gossips about them. Help them to see it is O.K. to share your own secret elsewhere, but not another's. You can use example questions:

> "How did you feel when someone told another person what you were going to give them for their birthday?"
> "Was a surprise ever spoiled for you due to someone's sharing?"
> "Do you think gossip always hurts people?"

The norms should be posted in a prominent place and reviewed each time tribes meet. **Take care to observe them yourself.** If you do occasionally break one of the ground rules, encourage the class to bring this to your attention. Accept such reminders graciously, without defensiveness. Children are great rule enforcers, and in time, they are the ones who will monitor the norms for your class. **Peer supported behaviors are more readily internalized than teacher enforced rules.**

Giving the Instructions:

After acknowledging the norms, describe the activity that the full group will be doing. Be as concise as possible whenever giving activity instructions. Let the group know how much time will be allowed for completion of the group activity and state why we are doing it. For example, if you are using the inclusion activity "Three Tribles," you might say:

"The pictures of the three little Tribles give each person a chance to say which Trible I feel like this morning. It is important to know how we feel before we go to work. It will take us about twenty minutes to hear from everyone."

Initiating the Sharing:

It is best if you, the facilitator, initiates sharing by saying something like, "O.K., I'll start. This morning I feel like the middle Trible . . . quiet but not excited. I think I was up rather late last night." Then, "let's go around the circle starting with you Dustin, then Courtney, Colin and Jose."

Remind them of their Right to Pass when they seem tongue-tied or embarrassed. When a child does pass, openly acknowledge her with a nod or smile to convey it is all right. She hasn't let you down, and you can facilitate another opportunity to share in a second time around the circle.

Keeping Things Moving:

It is best not to comment on anyone's contribution during the activity itself. Some brief nonverbal acknowledgement is usually sufficient. You can make mental notes on things you want to bring up later. However, if someone gets put down by another child or by the group (derisive laughter, groans etc.) deal with the incident in a direct but matter-of-fact way. Remind people of the No Put-Down rule. Go around the circle once, and then give people who passed a second chance to share.

Encouraging Follow-up:

After everyone has had a turn, allow time for questions and comments. Ask people to speak directly to one another, and to use first names. Model this by saying: "Lisa, I liked it when you talked about your hope of becoming an artist."

You can initiate this interaction by referring to some of those "mental notes" you were keeping. Do not dominate the discussion yourself. Just facilitate and clarify as needed.

Asking Discussion and Reflection Questions:

We use the terms "discussion" and "reflection" to describe the kinds of post-activity questions that need to be asked so that learning evolves from the group experience.

> **Discussion** questions are focused on the **content or subject** of the activity. They are impersonal, factual and therefore the safest level of questioning.
>
> Examples:
> "What was the main idea that your group discussed?"
> "What similarities or differences did you notice in what people thought about the idea?"

The purpose of discussion questions is to help people develop the confidence to speak up and express themselves in a group setting.

> **Reflection** questions are focused on personal learnings or felt experiences during the activity. They center on the expression of individual feelings, the group's interactions and the quality of the time just spent together.
>
> Examples:
> "How were you feeling while you were waiting for your turn in the group?"
> "Did you feel that people were really listening to you?"
> "How did your group decide who would be the recorder?"

The purpose of Reflection questions is to give children opportunities to become aware of their own attitudes and feelings in the midst of an experience. **Time out** for "reflection" helps to ground personal learnings and encourages taking responsibility for situations in which we find ourselves. It develops the capacity of introspection which is essential to becoming self-directed in life.

A short-hand way to remember the difference between these two types of questions might be:

Discussion questions focus on **content**
Reflection questions focus on **personal experience and feelings**

Discussion questions are asked first after each activity . . . then reflection questions. Pay attention to your own feelings while observing the tribes working together; appropriate reflection questions will soon evolve as easily as content discussion questions do for us as teachers. We want to emphasize that the suggested questions on the activity pages in this book may not be appropriate for your own class. There simply are no "sure-fire" questions that are right for every group situation and cultural population. Your own intuition, creativity and judgment are needed to draw out the most important learnings from all group activities.

Encouraging Appreciation:

In addition to discussing and reflecting upon the experience of each activity, you have the wonderful opportunity to significantly increase student self-esteem throughout the Tribes process. Always give a a few minutes at the end of any group involvement to ask people to express appreciation to each other. Earlier we gave suggested sentence-starters that you can use to encourage positive statements. It is tremendously meaningful to hear one's peers acknowledge special qualities, skills and caring behaviors that one has given in the group's time together.

We need also to encourage people to affirm themselves by inviting members to share their pride of a job well done, their positive leadership or special contribution. It's O.K. to have children brag! To believe in oneself is to have high self-regard . . . to feel empowered, competent and confident of meeting the challenges in an ever-widening world.

Here is a quick summary of the steps to be used in leading any full group activity:

Leading a Full Group Activity . . . Step By Step

1. Teach and Model the Norms
- Involve students in defining what they need for good group environment.
- Have the norms posted where everyone can see them.
- Have the norms reviewed each group session.
- Model the ground rules congruently yourself.

2. Give the instructions
- Briefly describe the activity and its purpose.
- Give instructions simply and concisely.
- Tell people how much time will be allowed for completion of the activity or task.

3. Initiate the sharing
- Begin with yourself.
- Let all know who will be next . . . which way the circle will go.
- Make it O.K. "to pass."

4. Keep things moving
- Withhold your own comments on what children share.
- Repeat instructions as needed.
- Deal with put-downs or lack of attentive listening as needed.
- Give passers a second opportunity to share.

5. Encourage follow-up
- Ask people to speak directly to one another.
- Encourage people to use first names.
- Facilitate and clarify as needed.

6. Ask discussion and reflection questions
- Begin with discussion questions focusing on content.
- Continue with reflection questions focusing on feelings and experience.
- Ask "what" rather than "how" people felt.
- Follow your own intuition.
- Wind things up when people feel bored or restless.

7. Encourage appreciation
- Use sentence-starters.
- Be a good role-model.

Using Temporary Small Groups to Build Community

Full group activities are not the only way to build community and promote initial inclusion in the classroom. The major disadvantages of the large community circle format is that each child must spend more time listening than talking which leads to restlessness and dependency upon the teacher to maintain control. The community circle, like traditional teaching methods, is still teacher-centered rather than student-centered. Again, if you study the Tribes Trail Map, you will notice that temporary sub-groups also are used to help people feel included. Prior to the formation of longer term membership tribes (or learning groups), multiple experiences in "trial" groups helps people to become comfortable. While your students are working together in these practice groups (without you facilitating directly), you can observe how different combinations of children get along together. This will be valuable information when you are ready to assign students to their permanent tribes.

Building Community Creatively

Please do not feel limited to the tribal activities in this book when it comes to developing a sense of community among all your students. Use your own intuition, sense of timing and creativity to create or adapt activities so they are appropriate. The duration of time that an activity will take for your class is not necessarily the same as noted on the activities in Chapter VIII of this book. You must make allowance for younger children, special education classes, age level and class size.

There are an abundance of good inclusion activities in other books. Skits, games, outdoor activities . . . really any class activity in which people are working or playing together cooperatively can contribute to class inclusion. As you become comfortable with the Tribes process, we know you like other teachers will accumulate your own fine repertoire. Always make sure that the positive norms are being observed and that you make time for discussion, reflection and sharing appreciation.

"WHEN IN DOUBT, FOCUS ON FEELINGS . . .
SURFACE WHATEVER MAY BE GOING ON."

4

BUILDING
TRIBES

4 Building Tribes

They speak to one another in hushed whispers. Eyes glance from face to face in silent scrutiny. There is but one question in the mind of each child as the class files in from morning recess. Quickly they take their seats. All eyes are on the teacher, who is carefully examining some papers on her desk. Could those be the membership lists? The teacher looks up. She explains that there are thirty pieces of cardboard hidden around the classroom and that each piece has someone's name on it. The pieces fit together to form five large round puzzles. She tells the students that each person is to find his or her own piece and then find the others whose pieces match. Thirty wide-eyed, giggling children scurry from cabinets to bookcase, from bulletin board to rabbit cage. Within five minutes there are five groups huddled around completed "people puzzles," getting to know one another in the fine tradition of Tribes.

* * * *

Yes, after building community inclusion and getting your students familiar with the norms of the Tribes Program, the time has come for you to assign people to long-term membership learning groups . . . tribes. The material in this chapter will enable you to do just that. You will learn how to:

- determine when your class is ready for tribes
- introduce your class to the tribes concept
- achieve sociometric balance in assigning tribe membership
- use a tribal activity to announce and form tribes
- build tribe inclusion
- lead activities in tribes
- teach and use "I-Messages"
- facilitate the "transfer of responsibility" to small groups
- resolve group issues that commonly occur in small groups

Is Your Class Ready for Tribes?

After several weeks of community activities, you may start asking yourself in the wee hours of the night whether the time has come to take the next step. Your class is probably ready to form long term learning groups when you can say "yes" to the following questions:

Readiness for Tribes

1. Do they understand and respect the norms (most of the time)?

2. Do they know each other's name?

3. Can you identify the leaders, isolates, friendships and possible behavior problems?

4. Have they had successful multiple experiences working in various "trial tribes" or practice groupings?

5. Do you feel ready to "take the plunge?" (Aw, c'mon!)

Introducing the Concept

One day when you are feeling good and things are going smoothly, take a few minutes to talk about everyone's experience of being together not only in the large community circle but many smaller groupings. Tell them that now the class is ready to become members of longer term learning groups. Of course, this announcement will start everyone wondering just who their tribe members will be. Assure everyone that they will have the opportunity to tell you who they would like to have in their group, and that you will make sure each person is in a tribe with at least one chosen friend. Tell the class that the reason for forming tribes is not only to make **new** friends but for people to be able to help each other work on curricula throughout the year.

You may want to spend some time talking about what it is like to be a member of a group, club, family or team; perhaps have them discuss the purposes of various social systems. You may ask discussion questions like:

> "Why do people want to join different groups?"
> "Have you ever been in a club or group with a few people who became very special to you?"
> "Why do people live and even work together in small groups?"

You don't need to "sell" the concept, or come on with too much enthusiasm: "Oh, boys and girls, tribes will be **such fun!**" Simply tell them what they can expect and answer their questions. Use your attentive listening skills to let them know you are hearing their concerns. Some may feel excitement at this point, others anxiety. Do what you can to help them become interested and invested in the idea of belonging to a small group of their classmates.

Sociometry Made Easy

The guidelines for assigning people to tribes are important:

1. Assign no less then five and no more than six members to each tribe.
2. Balance the number of boys and girls in each group.
3. Distribute "leader" types among all the tribes.
4. Distribute "isolates" (shy, less social, disruptive etc.) among all groups.
5. Be certain that each person has at least one chosen friend in his/her tribe.

Here is a step-by-step process that you can use to achieve a sociometric balance in your classroom groups, without using any cumbersome instruments.

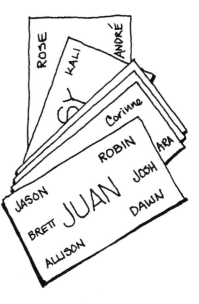

Six Friends

1. Give each child a 5″ × 8″ index card.

2. Ask each child to print his/her name in the center of the card.

3. Ask each child to print the names of six others that he/she would like to have in a tribe. (Kindergarten and first grade children may need help with this.)

4. Collect all the cards. Remind your students that they will each be in a tribe with at least one identified friend, but that it is not possible to be with all those listed.

5. Assuming that you will have five tribes in your classroom, select the cards belonging to five "leader" types who best model positive social behavior. Spread these cards out in front of you on the floor or a large work table.

6. Next select the cards belonging to five students who tend to exhibit less appropriate behavior. Place one next to each of the cards from step #5.

7. Add four or five more cards to each group, making sure that each card you add has a name on it that is requested by one of those already in the grouping.

8. Make any adjustments necessary to achieve boy-girl balance.

9. Check one more time to be sure that each card is still matched with a "friend."

10. Congratulations! You have just formed your tribes!

The "Six Friends" method of assigning members enables you to match or separate children to achieve the best mix of relationships. It has the added advantage of allowing your students some influence in determining who will be in which tribe.

Forming Tribes

Once you have determined the membership for the classroom groups, set a date for announcing tribes to your class. Let them know a day or two in advance so that anticipation can build. When "T-Day" arrives, provide an exciting way for people to discover who is in which tribe. Here are the directions for the activity described in the beginning of the chapter:

People Puzzles

1. Begin with sheets of posterboard, one for each tribe.
2. Cut each piece into five or six irregular shaped pieces of comparable size.
3. Print a child's name with a felt marker on each section. Make sure that all the members of a tribe are included in the same People Puzzle.
4. Hide the pieces around the classroom before school, during lunch or recess.
5. Instruct the children to look for their own names only, and to leave other children's pieces where they find them.
6. Tell them to match their pieces with others until all the People Puzzles have been completed.
7. Lead a discussion in which everyone has a chance to share how it was to assemble their tribes in this way.

You can, of course, invent other ways to form tribes. The activity called "Barnyard Babble" would be more appropriate for older students, providing an hilarious experience in discovering their fellow tribe members and finding inclusion together.

After the groups have been formed, state that people will remain in these groups for at least one month; then we will see how everyone is getting along. This defuses the inevitable remarks that "I wanted to have someone else in my tribe!" Once we did a survey to learn how many new Tribe teachers actually had to alter the membership of the groups; it was determined that those who had people stay in the same group for at least three weeks did not need to make **any** changes in the membership. The secret is that by then the process of inclusion has been successful in providing a sense of belonging and trust. People have forgotten about wanting a particular friend . . . they have made four or five new friends who they like, trust and do not want to leave.

Building Tribe Inclusion

Remember that Tribes Trail theory rap that we did back in Chapter II? Well, here is where your understanding of it really moves into application. Although your class has spent several weeks in activities that have built "community inclusion," each person now senses the same initial anxieties as new groups are formed.

It is essential that you facilitate a series of activities that will help people **present who they are, what they do well, and what they want their group to be like. They are not ready to work on curricula together unless inclusion and trust have intentionally been developed.** Disruptive behavior in classrooms (taking away from your time to teach) occurs because children do not feel **included.** And if you remember your lesson in Chapter II, you'll recall that:

> "A way to become included is to grab influence."

That's what plagues teachers throughout the day and school year. Anti-social behavior gains attention meaning "someone notices me and cares". . . it is a way to feel included and of importance in the midst of many others. The Tribes Program decreases behavior problems in schools simply because everyone is included in a positive peer learning group.

It's a fine idea on the day before the new tribes are to be announced to invite people in your class to bring something special from home to share at the first meeting of their new tribe. Tell them it should have special meaning, perhaps an award, or something they have made. Sharing such treasures on the first day will help each student introduce himself and quickly promote a sense of positive energy in the group.

Activities that Build Tribe Inclusion

Though we have said it before and will say it again, it is important that you select inclusion activities geared to the interests, age level and culture of your particular class. Do read the preface to the Activities section before leaping into using them. Hopefully, you are involved in an in-service training for the Tribes Program, and will experience many good activities that can be easily adapted to your class. Some of the favorites for elementary school students include:

Name Game	Wishful Thinking
Spider Web	Silhouettes
Brainstorming	Warm Fuzzybag
Kitchen Kapers	Campaign Manager
Tribe Mimes	Interview Circle
What's My Bag	Zoo Stories

One teacher advises, "You need to be as flexible and creative as you are with all other curriculum!"

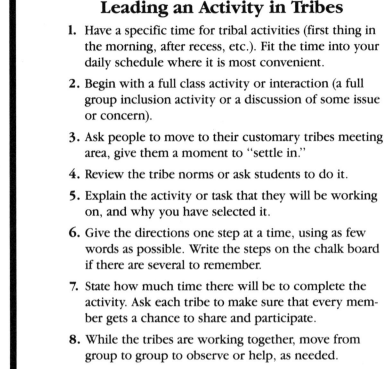

Leading an Activity in Tribes

1. Have a specific time for tribal activities (first thing in the morning, after recess, etc.). Fit the time into your daily schedule where it is most convenient.

2. Begin with a full class activity or interaction (a full group inclusion activity or a discussion of some issue or concern).

3. Ask people to move to their customary tribes meeting area, give them a moment to "settle in."

4. Review the tribe norms or ask students to do it.

5. Explain the activity or task that they will be working on, and why you have selected it.

6. Give the directions one step at a time, using as few words as possible. Write the steps on the chalk board if there are several to remember.

7. State how much time there will be to complete the activity. Ask each tribe to make sure that every member gets a chance to share and participate.

8. While the tribes are working together, move from group to group to observe or help, as needed.

9. When time is up, ask people to move with their tribes back into the full group, or to stay where they are and pay attention as the whole class listens to each tribe.

10. Ask each tribe to report on what they did and how it went. With older children it is sometimes preferable to have them discuss and reflect upon their experience as a tribe, before asking them to report to the full group.

11. Ask people to take time to make statements of appreciation to one another either in the full group or in their tribes.

Transferring Responsibility

One of the major objectives of the Tribes Program is to "call forth" responsibility and positive leadership qualities in children. This means that an intentional transfer of control needs to be made from the teacher to the tribe, and from the tribe to its individuals. It means that sensitive teachers look for opportunities to have the tribes function independently. Here are some of the ways that you can transfer responsibility:

- stay out of tribal activities as much as possible;
- encourage tribe members to remind each other about the norms;
- when students ask you a question, refrain from answering it; turn it back to the class or tribe, asking "does anyone have the answer?"
- ask tribe members to help with passing out materials and reporting back to the full class;
- have tribes help you with attendance by reporting any absent members and helping returning members with missed assignments;
- have the class make a list of classroom maintenance tasks; and ask tribes to each assume one for a period of time.
- have the tribes plan parties, field trips, parent involvement and other class activities;
- ask tribes for suggestions to improve lesson plans, academic projects and learning environment.

Observing the Process

Admittedly, it can feel strange to be in the background while your tribes tackle a challenging, engrossing activity. This, however, is not a time to sit idly by, or to catch up on correcting those arithmetic papers! During these periods when your busy tribes cease to "need" you, you become the "process observer," paying attention not only to individual behaviors, but also to the subtle indicators of interpersonal dynamics. Following is a list of some of the dynamics that you can observe while your tribes are working together. You will identify many more indicators as you learn to relax and watch the amazing process unfold.

Process Observation Checklist

1. **How are people sitting?**
   - Are they in a neat circle, or are some people sitting back from the group?
   - Are they leaning forward attentively, or are they slouching, sprawling or "laying back"?

2. **How are people participating?**
   - Are a few doing all the talking or is participation balanced?
   - Are people lively and animated, or lethargic and tentative?
   - Is everyone focused on what is happening, or are side conversations taking place?
   - Are people "passing"?

3. **How are people taking care of one another?**
   - Are they listening to one another?
   - Are put-downs happening? If so, are they being confronted by group members?
   - Are disagreements being resolved in satisfying ("win-win") ways?
   - Is kindness and cooperation being demonstrated? Is appreciation being expressed?
   - Is the group drawing in the isolates?

4. **How are people feeling and behaving?**
   - Are they smiling and/or laughing?
   - Are people touching one another (versus punching, poking or pinching)?
   - Is your "intuitive response" one of warmth and relaxation or anxiety and tension?

5. **Are they working well on task or curricula?**
   - Who has assumed leadership?
   - Are the slow learners included?
   - Do they seem mindful of the goal to complete the assignment on time?

6. **What is happening for you?**

7. **Other?**

Facilitating the Process

So what happens when you observe breakdowns in the process? Let's use an example. You have given your fourth grade tribes the activity, To Build a Better Bathtub, so that they will learn about brainstorming. Your ultimate purpose is to have them use the same process later in a history lesson. One recorder in each tribe is furiously attempting to write down all the ideas being voiced by tribe members. While observing the behaviors in each tribe, you notice that one of the recorders is really having a hard time getting all the information on paper. People are saying things like "Hey, you left mine out. Slow poke!" Your impulse is to "take charge," to stride over and say something like, "C'mon, give Sara a break! You, Tyler, why don't you be a second recorder and help Sara out; and no more put downs! Don't you remember the norms?"

Instead, you take a deep breath and reflect on all that is going on. You observe that only two students, Jill and Colin, are really "into" the activity. They are leaning forward and putting forth many ideas. The other tribe members are sitting back rather apathetically waiting for the time to run out.

What are your alternatives other than intervening directively?
You could do nothing, in which case the situation would either:

1. Stay the same.
2. Get better (someone might volunteer to help Sara out, or Sara might ask for help).
3. Get worse (Sara might break down in tears or anger; a huge argument might erupt).

As a fourth alternative, you could assign reflection questions after the activity is completed, questions that would help tribes become aware of, and take responsibility for the behavior of group members. **Example:** "O.K. folks, before we hear about the activity, I'd like you to take about five minutes to discuss these questions in your tribes. And please limit your comments to these questions."

- Were the norms honored?
- Did everyone participate? Why or why not?
- What was it like being the recorder?

You might choose to write these questions on the blackboard or butcher paper.

"But," you exclaim, "why make all the tribes go through this when only one tribe had the problem?" Good question! In this case, the suggested "strategy" might accomplish the following:

- Sara's tribe, in addition to exploring their own behaviors, would learn from the other tribes how they dealt with the same or similar issues.
- The other tribes would certainly benefit from discussing these questions and reflecting on their own process together.
- By observing the responses of Sara's tribe during the reflection assignment, you would have additional data to use in deciding what specific work needs to be done with this tribe alone.
- The full group discussion that follows the reflection time will certainly yield valuable information in a variety of related areas.

Of course, if Sara's tribe does not report on the behavior you have observed, you should comment on it at this time. Not to do so would be interpreted by the members of this tribe as an indication you were not paying attention, or that you did not think it was important.

Keeping Your Purpose and Role in Mind

The Tribe process and the activities that you choose to use in your classroom have but one overall purpose:

> to assure children's academic achievement and social development by intentionally creating an environment that builds individual self-esteem, caring behaviors and the capacity to work cooperatively (rather than competitively) with others.

The tribe activities are not "time-fillers or unnecessary frills for the classroom," but are meaningful experiences teaching children how to reflect upon and manage their increasingly complex relational worlds. Your role is to **facilitate** (meaning "to make easy") their cooperative working process. As the teacher-facilitator you are the "caretaker" of the classroom social climate. Again, as stated many times earlier, this means modeling the norms, gently but firmly, and insisting they be respected throughout the school day. These ground rules are the key to the positive learning environment that assures academic achievement.

Negative Feelings and Issues

We have discussed the importance of caring communication, but this does not mean that angry and negative feelings are not allowed. On the contrary, negative feelings and issues must be acknowledged and dealt with in an open and constructive manner.

I-Messages[17]

To help your students express feelings and confront inappropriate behavior without putting judgment on others, it is important for you to teach and model the use of "I-Messages. An I-Message is a statement of the speaker's feelings in response to a situation or the behavior or others. The statement, unlike a "You-Message," does not convey judgment nor is it a "put-down." The examples below are helpful in delineating between the two types of statements:

You-Message:
"You dummy, you spilled paint all over my shirt. You make me so angry."

I-Message:
"Cary, I'm very angry that paint was spilled all over my shirt."

In the first example, Cary was rudely put-down and held solely responsible for the incident. In the second example, the speaker took the responsibility for his feelings, stated them in strong terms . . . but did not put the blame on Cary.

I-Messages	**You-Messages**
• State and "own the speaker's feelings	• Hold another person responsible for speaker's feelings.
• Focus on behavior, not personal judgments.	• Make personal judgments; put people down.

The purpose of an I-Message is to communicate feelings in such a way that the other person is not forced to defend herself or avoid the situation. The impact of the You-Message blames, shames or intimidates the other person. It causes the other person to become resistant. The recipient of a You-Message has been labeled "bad or wrong," and she will be unable to meet the speaker half-way towards possible resolution of their difficulty. Worst of all, You-Messages kill self-esteem.

We need also to be aware of You-Messages that "masquerade" as I-Messages. For example: "I feel that you are always a nuisance," is a disguised put-down, a You-Message because:

1. No feelings are stated or owned even though the speaker says "I feel" (he really means "I think").
2. The phrase, "You are always a nuisance" is a judgment, implying that the person is bad or incapable of being different.

In teaching people how to use I-Messages, it is helpful to write this formula on the chalkboard:

"I feel _____(name the feeling)
when _____(describe the situation or behavior)

It is important to give many examples:

"I feel **confused** when I'm **shouted at**."
"I feel **sad** when I hear someone hurts his **cat**."
"I feel **scared** when I'm yelled at."

I-Messages are also a very powerful way to communicate **positive feelings**:

"I feel **happy** when I receive a compliment."
"I feel **excited** when we **meet** in **tribes**."
"I feel **glad** when **the bell rings**."

The I-Message is a tricky concept to master, even though it seems quite simple at first. This is another instance where you need to be an appropriate **role model**. Your students may not completely understand the concept of the I-Message, but with your example and a little practice, they too will begin to use them.

Let's suppose that many people in your class are upset with four students who seem to be more disruptive, upset group activities or in one way or another claim too much attention. You have encouraged people to use I-Messages in their tribes to communicate their feelings at the time of any upsetting events. You have also spent some separate time with these students trying to glean clues concerning their antisocial behavior and to build more inclusion to yourself. Knowing that the message of peers to each other is still more powerful in altering behavior, you decide to use a community circle technique "Resent, Request and Appreciate."

RRA Instructions

1. Have the class seated in a large circle.

2. Explain that in this activity, people will have an opportunity either to ask for or give someone three I-Messages: "I resent . . . , I request . . . , I appreciate." Give examples, using yourself as a possible RRA recipient. Example: "Mrs.Gibbs, I **resent** it when you interrupt me. I **request** that you let me finish what I am saying. I **appreciate** your sense of humor in our class."

3. Stress that people have the right to pass, and that people can also pass on accepting RRA's.

4. Explain that when someone agrees to accept an RRA, he/she also agrees to repeat it back to the person who said it to him. ("Sara, you resent it when I interrupt you, you request that I let you finish talking, and you appreciate my sense of humor.")

5. The "repeating back" is the key to this process for three reasons:
   • It insures that the recipient has heard what has been said to her.
   • It gives the sender the satisfaction of knowing she was heard, which invariably results in her having greater respect for the recipient.
   • It permits one to give feedback to another concerning behavior and yet recognizes positive qualities at the same time.

You really have to stay on top of this activity to make sure that:

- everyone's right to pass is respected;
- no put-downs occur;
- RRA's are reflected back to the sender; and
- true statements of appreciation occur every time.

If you can just keep it safe, the class will usually do the rest and many disruptive behaviors will melt away.

Knowing When to "Take Charge"

Even the most sensitive, caring teacher needs to be directive at times, and I-Messages are seldom appropriate for this. For example, you encounter one child hitting another. An immediate statement of "Stop that this instant!" is a much more appropriate reaction than: "I feel unhappy when you hit Aaron and I would like you to stop."

Dealing effectively with anti-social or inappropriate behavior means knowing when to encourage children to use I-Messages with one another, when to use an I-Message yourself, when to be directive and "take charge." The social climate in your classroom and your success with the the Tribes Program will be greatly influenced by the way in which conflict and angry feelings are routinely expressed and resolved by you and your students. Conflict management techniques usually all boil down to:

- owning feelings,
- recognizing how my behavior affects others
- stating expectations clearly,
- acknowledging and respecting different points of view, feelings, and values; and
- commitment to a resolution in which both parties "win" and nobody loses.

Resolving Group Issues

As a tribes teacher, your willingness to acknowledge, discuss and resolve group issues in a caring, process-based manner will result in growth and learning for you and your students. It is inevitable that all groups of people living, playing or working together will experience many predictable issues. The chart on the following page gives an overview of typical questions that come up during any group's development and gives suggestions for you the facilitator to resolve many situations. Among the more common issues that may happen in your classroom are the following:

TRIBES ISSUE CHART

	ISSUES	QUESTIONS/FEELINGS	YOU, THE FACILITATOR, NEED TO:
INCLUSION	Presentation of Self	"Will I like this group?" "How will they get to know me?"	Be directive and provide structure. Introduce activities that permit each person to share who he/she is, what feelings, skills, qualities, resources he/she offers.
		"I feel nervous with all these people."	Have people work in dyads and triads, which feel safer and less threatening. Assign art and crafts projects that place focus on the task, not on individuals.
		"Will they listen to me?" "Will they put me down?"	Teach communications and listening skills. Make sure that people respect the Tribes norms, especially No Put-Downs.
	Expectations and Needs	"Will we finish by 3 o'clock?" "May we work outside today?" "Can you all help me with a problem I am having?"	Provide opportunities for each member to state wants, needs and expectations during the time the group spends together.
	Acknowledgement	"Will they like me?" "Do I dare tell someone I think he/she is a nice person?" "Does anyone else feel the same way I feel?"	Be a good "role model" by giving and receiving appreciation easily Provide opportunities for people to exchange statements of appreciation and good feelings. Ask reflection questions that encourage people to share thoughts and feelings about coming together as a group.
INFLUENCE	Me versus the Group	"Will my opinions be respected?"	Provide activities that help people define and state individual differences.
	Goals	"What are we to accomplish together?"	Introduce techniques that elicit input from each member in defining group goals. Model and encourage acceptance of all ideas before choosing group goals.
	Decision-Making	"How can we reach agreement?"	Introduce techniques for group decision-making, e.g., sticker-voting. Consensus Decision-Making activity.
	Conflict	"How can we work this out?"	Introduce conflict resolution techniques, e.g., active listening, I-Messages, role-reversal. Assist group members in reaching "win-win" solutions.
	Leadership & Authority	"Do we need a leader?"	Encourage rotation of leadership roles. Urge "natural leaders" to draw out more passive members.
		"I resent it when someone tries to tell us what to do."	Ask reflection questoins that help members discuss and resolve leadership problems. Use conflict resolution techniques as needed.
AFFECTION	Creativity: Individual & Group	"I feel good about my abilities."	Recognize individuals for unique achievements and self-direction; encourage group members to do so with one another.
	Cooperation	"Our group really works well together."	Assign group tasks that requre innovation, cooperation and creativity.
	Achievement	"We really did a great job!"	Assign group academic projects: all group members receive the same grade or reward.
		"What shall we tackle next?"	Use groups for "peer teaching," problem-solving, planning and fun! Be alert for inclusion and influence issues that come up; support the group in resolving them.
		"I really like our group!"	Enjoy, and feel proud of yourself! They may never remember your sensitive guidance, but **you** know how it all happened!

1. Lack of Inclusion

Early in the tribe building process, some people may be "passing" all the time and others seem to be isolated and not participating. This type of behavior is usually an indication that some people feel unsafe with their groups. Suggestions:

- Discuss the reasons why some people are not participating and then have the tribes brainstorm ideas for including people more.
- Have people work in pairs during an activity. Match a shy child with a more confident out-going one.
- Make sure that you are using appropriate inclusion activities. (Try: "Interview Circle" in tribes).
- Spend some time with the isolate. Learn his/her special interests and talents; encourage him/her to share them with the tribe.
- Assign the isolate a leadership role or task in the tribe.
- Make sure that the norms are being honored so that the environment becomes **safe**.

2. "I don't like my tribe."

A person who feels uncomfortable in his group may say things like:

"I don't like the people in my tribe."
"I get bored in my tribe."
"People in my tribe are dumb."
"I want to be in Cary's tribe."

Rather than trying to talk the child out of his/her complaint, use your listening skills to find out what is really going on. Suggestions:

- Enlist the help of the tribe to give the person more inclusion.
- Gear some tribe activities to his/her interests and abilities.
- Ask the person to "hang in" for two or three weeks with the tribe; by this time things usually work themselves out.
- In some extreme cases, it may be advisable to transfer a child to another tribe, or to provide him/her with something to do alone while tribes are meeting. These last two are "last resort" measures, not to be considered unless all else fails.

3. Including new tribe members

When a new person enters your class after tribes have been formed, it is important to make an effort to give her a special welcome. For example, a new girl named Robin shows up at school on Monday. She is given a short tour of the school; then she is introduced to her new teacher and classmates. The teacher may enlist the help of one or two students to explain to the newcomer what tribes are all about. Later in the morning, Robin experiences the Tribe Adoption Ceremony.

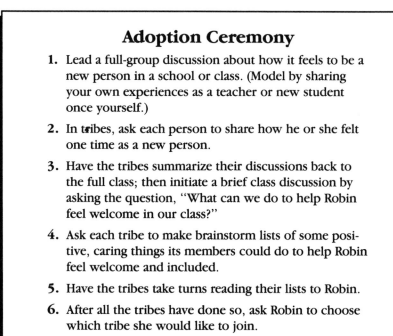

Adoption Ceremony

1. Lead a full-group discussion about how it feels to be a new person in a school or class. (Model by sharing your own experiences as a teacher or new student once yourself.)

2. In tribes, ask each person to share how he or she felt one time as a new person.

3. Have the tribes summarize their discussions back to the full class; then initiate a brief class discussion by asking the question, "What can we do to help Robin feel welcome in our class?"

4. Ask each tribe to make brainstorm lists of some positive, caring things its members could do to help Robin feel welcome and included.

5. Have the tribes take turns reading their lists to Robin.

6. After all the tribes have done so, ask Robin to choose which tribe she would like to join.

During this activity, have Robin stay close to you and observe the process. If you decide that you should choose which tribe Robin belongs in, you can still ask your tribes to come up with creative ideas for helping her to feel welcome and included. Hundreds of parents have expressed their great appreciation to tribal schools that use this ceremony. In a very transient society, it is wonderful to have your child come home the first day and say, "I belong to a tribe now and the kids were so nice to me!"

4. Combating "Put-Downs"

If you find that in spite of your most heroic efforts, people are still serving up lots of "cold prickly" put-down statements, you may want to take some remedial measures. In terms of group dynamics, children who put down others are attempting to gain recognition and influence. Suggestions:

- Have the tribes make lists of put-down statements, then share how it feels to receive them.
- Initiate an "anti-put-down" campaign.
- Challenge the clever prickly "experts" to create imaginative ways to show appreciation for their group members.
- Provide lots of opportunities for statements of appreciation. Activities like Campaign Manager and Self-esteem cards are especially useful.
- Be a good role model, both in giving and accepting statements of appreciation. Just make sure you are honest at all times . . . kids can spot a "plastic fuzzy" a block away!

5. "Let's form new tribes!"

If your students begin agitating to change tribes, it is probably an indication that you need to do more full-group inclusion, especially small-group activities with children who are not in the same tribe. Suggestions:

- Remind your students that they will remain in the same groups for at least one month, before we decide on any changes.
- Combine two tribes for an activity like Interview Circle.
- Introduce full-group activities that focus on people's different opinions: Thumbs Up-Thumbs Down and Put Yourself on the Line.

We want to emphasize once more that membership in tribes needs to remain as constant as possible throughout the school year. It is this on-going membership factor that builds the peer support system and positive learning environment.

There really is no way to anticipate and address all of the issues that may arise as you initiate cooperative learning groups in your classroom. The next chapter, Encouraging Responsible Behavior, presents ways to handle **issues of influence** and using groups for **problem-solving**. It is very important for you to get together with other teachers who are using the Tribe Program, so that you can share ideas, generate creative activities, and be a supportive group for each other.

5

ENCOURAGING
RESPONSIBLE BEHAVIOR

5
Encouraging Responsible Behavior

Some of your sixth graders have been picking on little kids during recess and lunch periods, and the principal has asked you to deal with the bullies. You ask your class to meet in tribes, and you lead them through a "guided fantasy" recalling the time when they too were in kindergarten. You then ask them to share how they felt as kindergartners when they were around older children who teased them. Without naming names you tell your students that the principal has asked the class to come up with some ideas on making the playground a safer, happier place for little kids. You ask your tribes to brainstorm, then prioritize their suggestions. After a full-group discussion, everyone agrees on several things the class will do to solve the problem.

*   *   *   *

This vignette illustrates how tribes can help to manage behavior problems that occur even outside the tribal setting. In the example (which really happened) without being confronted directly, the "bullies" became aware that their aggressive behavior was not approved by their peers. By participating in the group's problem-solving, these students become part of the solution.

In the last two chapters we have been concerned with the process of getting tribes "off the ground." Now that your tribes are meeting on a regular daily basis, and some of the initial inclusion issues have been resolved, we will explore some ways that the groups themselves can be a positive influence on behavior and learning.

The material in this chapter will provide you with some strategies that:

- encourage children to express and respect different points of view;
- enable tribes to develop group decision-making and problem-solving skills;
- help students define and think through solutions to personal concerns;
- use positive peer influence to deal with inappropriate behavior.

Acknowledging Influence

You thought you had it "made." Your students have been in tribes for over a month and things are going great. No more agitating to change tribes. Almost no put-downs. And talk about working "independently" . . . one afternoon when they were working you realized you could have gone home at one o'clock and nobody (except perhaps the principal) would have missed you!

Then one morning your lovely smooth-running tribal classroom begins to get a little out of hand. Some of the people you counted on as positive role models are acting up. During tribe activities you notice many subtle and not-so-subtle indicators that disagreements are frequently occurring. I-Messages and attentive listening are helpful up to a point, but you know that something more is needed. Congratulations! The inclusion or "honeymoon" stage of the tribes process has run its course, and the **influence stage** has arrived! The new restlessness is but a sign that your students are comfortable with the group process, they feel safe, less dependent, and ready to initiate leadership. They need more opportunities to express their individuality, to influence the day-to-day operations of the classroom, to work responsibly on subject matter in their tribal learning groups. We have talked a lot about the transfer of responsibility from teacher to students. This is where it can really begin to happen as you set the necessary limits and introduce appropriate ways for students to become positive leaders. This is where the tribal classroom becomes a source of **positive peer power!**

Practicing Individuality and Respecting Differences

Although the founding principles of our democratic society are dedicated to the equality of all people no matter what their ethnicity, race, sex, religion, handicap or family background, schools (and other systems) still struggle to find ways to put the principles into practice. Whenever people feel a lack of respect or acceptance, it is inevitable that they will withhold their energy and unique resources from the group and fight to have inclusion and influence. They feel de-valued and without power in the midst of larger group or community.

In the Tribes process we define the **stage of influence** not as a time for people to fight for control or power, but as a stage where all help each other **feel valued**. Individual members learn to assert their diverse opinions, feelings and expectations within the group. Their unique talents, skills and backgrounds are shared and celebrated. As each comes to feel valued as a resource or leader in his/her own unique way, each begins to work more cooperatively and energetically.

Repeated practice at stating personal positions within a trusted peer group not only develops individuality but **self-esteem**. It takes courage based on self-esteem to take a stand saying, "I feel differently about this than the rest of you." Young people who are fortunate enough to experience this repeatedly through their childhood years will not be easily coerced in their adolescent years. They can do more than "just say no." They are able to make concious choices based upon their own values and beliefs.

Prior to working on subject matter (or along with it as described in the next chapter), the Tribes Program uses **influence activities** that help people gain a sense of uniqueness and value within their groups. Some to use are:

> Thumbs Up/Thumbs Down
> Put Yourself on the Line
> One, Two, Three

Let your own creativity also invent such activities as:

> Sharing my family's roots
> Cultural celebrations
> Ethnic lunch time
> School-family events

Every effort that you can make to have group members show appreciation for people's individual differences (culture, skills, talents, leadership expertise, values, opinions and beliefs) goes a long way towards developing that wonderful sense of value each one of us seeks.

> **"TO BE OF VALUE IS TO BE OF INFLUENCE"**

Group Decision-Making and Responsible Action

The **stage of influence** calls into question how the tribes should make decisions together and who should be responsible for what tasks. Reaching agreements even on simple things (such as, who will go up to the front of the room to report for our tribe?) often provokes group controversy.

One of the best ways to help people learn how to operate democratically is to allow them the **time to reflect on how a decision was made**.

After a group decision ask:

- How did your group decide who would be the leader?
- Did a few people tell the others what to do? How did that feel?
- Did you discuss how you would make the decision?
- Did you negotiate, take turns, select someone who could do the job well?

They also can practice working on problems that are fun and related to their different values and opinions. Some tribal activities that are appropriate are:

Space Pioneers
Dear Abby
Consensus Building

As your tribes become adept at working on problems together and reaching mutually satisfying solutions, give them real situations to deal with. For example:

- We only have four kick-balls to last us the year. How can we make sure that we don't lose any between now and June?
- How can we make sure that the plants get watered just the right amount each day?
- How can we share responsibility for feeding Benjamin Bunny and cleaning his cage?

Once a tribe has decided to work on something together, you can ask them to create an "action plan" with tasks to be done, persons responsible for each task and expected completion times. The action plan can be posted, reviewed daily and revised if necessary. The action plan becomes the "group contract" which clearly reminds people how they have promised to be responsible and accountable to one another.

Tribe Name: _____ **TRIBAL ACTION PLAN**		
Task	**Person Responsible**	**Completion Date**

Personal Problem-Solving . . . Choosing Responsible Behavior

Tribes provide an environment in which individual concerns, attitudes and problems may be thoughtfully explored. An essential part of each child's social development is the capacity to make responsible personal decisions. They need to learn how to make choices carefully and consciously, mindful of the probable outcomes for themselves and others. Here are two frameworks that can be used. The first one, "Let's Talk," is more suitable for discussions (with peers, teacher or parents); the second method, "Head, Heart and Feet" can be used to define questions for individual journal writing tasks, roll-play or discussions.

"Let's Talk"

1. **Define the problem, situation or concern:**
   Example:
   Whenever I go over to my friend's house after school, his mother is not home and he wants me to drink beer with him. I don't want to say "no" because he won't like me anymore.

2. **Repeat the problem back** (if in a discussion):
   Example:
   You mean that you think you have to drink with your friend or he won't be a friend anymore? Repeating back the problem usually brings elaboration.

3. **Think it through:**
   Example:
   • Would anybody lose respect for you if you drink with your friend?
   • Have you thought about the risks involved?
   • Are you certain your friend will not see you anymore?
   • Have you considered some alternatives?

4. **Look at both sides:**
   Example:
   • What would be the best things that would happen for you if you said "no"?
   • What would be the worst?

5. **Decide and act:**
   Example:
   • Having thought through the consequences, what is the most responsible choice you can make?
   • Are you willing to accept the possible consequences by acting on it?
   • If so, do it!

6. **Evaluate the outcome:**
   Example:
   • What happened? What did you learn?
   • Were you proud of your choice?
   • Would you make the same one again?

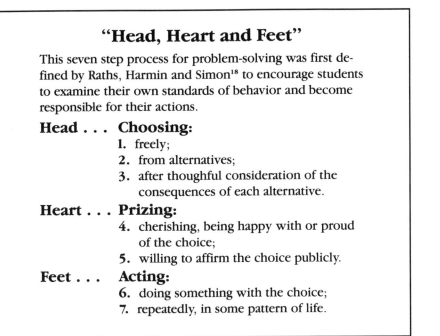

"Head, Heart and Feet"

This seven step process for problem-solving was first defined by Raths, Harmin and Simon[18] to encourage students to examine their own standards of behavior and become responsible for their actions.

Head . . . Choosing:
   1. freely;
   2. from alternatives;
   3. after thoughful consideration of the consequences of each alternative.

Heart . . . Prizing:
   4. cherishing, being happy with or proud of the choice;
   5. willing to affirm the choice publicly.

Feet . . . Acting:
   6. doing something with the choice;
   7. repeatedly, in some pattern of life.

The theory on which the process is based emphasizes that confusion results whenever our hearts (feelings) point one direction and our heads (thinking) indicate the opposite; in such a dilemma, our feet (action) are likely to do nothing or simply run off irresponsibly in any direction, unmindful of probable outcomes. Chosen behavior is more likely to be responsible constructive behavior.

Head, Heart and Feet correspond to the three domains of learning theory (cognitive, affective and psychomotor). When all three levels are working together, a person is behaving in a congruent manner. When there is conflict between the head, heart and feet, it can be said the person is experiencing dissonance.

Setting Goals and Making Individual Contracts

Our emphasis in the Tribes Program is to support children's social development in as many ways as possible in the school setting. We also want to help them **internalize** self-control to become self-directed individuals. This means giving them time to affirm healthy values and expectations that their families and they each have for themselves; and to define supportive steps toward achieving their personal goals.

One way to start working on goals is to have all tribe members

individually do the "Goal Storming" activity contained in Chapter VIII and then share their goals with another person in the tribe. Ask people to choose things about themselves that they would like to improve (skills, attitudes, behaviors or particular subject matter) during the next week. Short time durations are better than long term. As a way to model the activity, you might share your own list:

Teacher's List of Short Term Goals

1. To exercise ten minutes each morning this week.
2. To give up drinking coffee for at least one month.
3. To phone my friend tomorrow and apologize for forgetting her birthday.

After sharing lists, people can write **Personal Contracts** that can be signed by a peer who agrees to give encouragement and support. There is a form for the Personal Contract in the activity section. **Positive peer support is simply invaluable!**

The use of **Personal Journals** is also invaluable in helping people commit to personal goals, reflect upon their experiences and record important learnings, concerns or hopes. Personal Journals are respected as private documents that are shared only if a student chooses to do so. The activity Section (Chapter VIII) contains directions for using journals in classrooms.

Controlling Inappropriate Behavior

When people are involved together in finding a solution to a problem, they are more likely to accept responsibility for making the solution work.

The maxim is so simple but usually so difficult for teachers, parents and other adult caretakers to put into practice. Our immediate reaction to be the problem-solvers, "enforcers," or authorities inhibits the development of responsibility in our children. As much as teachers welcome the concept of positive peer influence, few have managed to challenge student ingenuity in this area. The vignette at the beginning of this chapter describes the successful outcome of a peer group problem-solving process. Here is the description of that process as applied to one school problem.

Step-by-Step Process for Group Problem-Solving

1. Lead your class in a guided fantasy which enables them to remember how they felt when they were in kindergarten and older children picked on them. Ask them to share their feelings in tribes; then have a full-group discussion.

2. Tell your class that the school needs to have some ways to manage the bullying-on-the-playground.

3. Pass out large sheets of paper. Ask tribes to brainstorm some ways that they, as older children, can bring a halt to the bullying whenever it begins to happen.

4. Ask each tribe to select their three best ideas or solutions.

5. Then compile a total class list from the individual tribe lists. Give each student three colored stickers to vote for his/her top choices; count blue stickers 15 points, red stickers 10 points, yellow stickers 5 points. Each child places a blue sticker next to his first choice, red on his second choice and yellow on the third. Adding up the sticker-points for each item yields the class decision. In this case, the top two or three ideas might be used.

6. Deal with the specifics of translating the good ideas into action. Example: one tribe may make a poster, another tribe may volunteer to be playground monitors, etc.

This simple decision-making process (called "Goalstorming" in the tribal activities section) enables a class to come to agreement quickly on issues that concern everyone. It can, of course, be used within a tribe setting just to solve its own issues apart from the total classroom.

You may wish to have your tribes brainstorm and come to agreement on the topic: "Behavior that bugs you." Just going through the process of identifying conduct that is not approved by the peer group often results in that behavior tapering off . . . positive peer pressure is powerful!

Taking Time to Mourn the Geranium

One of the keys to establishing and maintaining appropriate behavior norms in your classroom is taking time to discuss and reflect upon significant events that occur during the day. **The Geranium on the Windowsill Just Died, but Teacher, You Went Right On** (Albert Cullum, Quist Publishing Co., New York, 1971) is a funny, poignant and too-true commentary on a teacher who refused to acknowledge anything not in her lesson plan. There are many seemingly small events that are important during the day; they may be pivotal to gaining students full attention again on curricula. Examples:

- When someone loses a tooth, take time to discuss and celebrate.
- When someone feels she has been treated unfairly, take time out to discuss it.
- When the lesson you planned is going "over their heads," stop and perhaps say: "Boys and girls, it seems that this material on fractions isn't working out well for you. I feel frustrated too and would like to have your help to know what the problem might be. Let's talk about it!"

In some cases, you might have people meet in their tribes for a few minutes so that people have an opportunity to share their reactions. Taking time away from lessons to discuss and reflect upon unexpected events or feelings may set your schedule back temporarily, but in the long run, your students will realize that you respect their needs and they will begin to exhibit more mature responsible behavior. The time you save by not having to deal with so many discipline problems more than off-sets the time spent discussing important issues, events and personal reactions in the classroom.

> **"I AM A TEACHER . . . I TOUCH THE FUTURE!"**
>
> Susan Kovalik
> San Jose, California

6

COOPERATIVE
LEARNING GROUPS

6 Cooperative Learning Groups

You have heard about a classroom in which children themselves are helping to teach academic material to each other. This morning you decide to find out how this could ever work well.

Entering the classroom quietly you see that the teacher has the class sitting in a large community circle and is leading a discussion about sailing. "Tell me, girls and boys, how many of you have ever been on a sail boat?" A wave of excitement sweeps the room, and a flutter of hands appear. "Aaron," she asks, "can you tell us what it feels like?" Aaron describes his uncles's small boat, and a day when the wind on Lake Washington almost capsized it. Several other people want to tell their sailing experiences too. The sharing continues for a few more minutes, then the teacher asks the children to meet in their tribes.

She continues, "Let's imagine that you are about to go on a long sea voyage together and will be away from home for many months. Please think of one personal thing that you would want to take with you and then share that with your tribe. Remember to help each other listen carefully. You'll have five minutes to share."

After the sharing, the teacher invites each group to summarize their items. Then she says, "During the next few days we are going to learn about a very exciting sailing adventure. How many of you have heard of Christopher Columbus? (Several giggles . . . everyone raises hands). Well, I'm sure that we will learn a lot about Columbus that will amaze us. First, each of you will work in study groups to help you prepare the part of the lesson you will then teach to your tribe. Let's count off, one to six, and move to the study groups."

After tribal members rearrange themselves into six new study groups each containing five people, ten minutes is allowed for a brief inclusion activity so that people in the new groups are comfortable with each other. Each group is then given a different page of information concerning the voyage of Columbus. The teacher tells them they have thirty minutes to read and discuss the page together. As they work she moves from group to group, helping where needed.

When each study group has finished preparing its "lesson plan" all return to their respective tribes. Each child takes a turn at teaching the part of the lesson that he/she has been preparing in the study group. You are delighted to see the pride each experiences instructing the rest of the tribe. You notice how attentive and supportive everyone is. What might have been an irrelevant lesson has become an exciting event for this class.

*   *   *   *

The teacher portrayed in this example was trained in techniques that not only made the Christopher Columbus lesson come alive for her class but even helped the slower learners feel successful. The class was ready to work well in **cooperative learning groups** because a **positive classroom climate** and **cohesive groups** first had been developed through the Tribes process.

Schools across the nation are adopting cooperative group methods due to the comprehensive research[19] which shows that students who work in learning groups demonstrate an increase in their:

- retention of knowledge
- mastery of concepts and principles
- problem-solving skills
- creativity
- verbal skills
- ability to take another person's perspective

The effectiveness of group learning methods is assured when the Tribes process is used to structure the classroom's positive learning environment. The theoretical basis for this comes from studies showing that:

1. Children perform better on learning tasks when they are members of "high-cohesion" rather than "low cohesion" groups; and[20]
2. Students who feel comfortable with their peers utilize their academic abilities more fully than those who do not.[21]

"High cohesion" becomes a reality due to the inclusive process of the Tribes Program. The norms that build trust provide peer support to learn academic material; the social development activities provide a way to structure lesson plans. The next chapter on activities contains some examples of subject matter activities which Tribe teachers have designed.

This chapter will discuss and help you to:

- "personalize" the curriculum, and
- integrate cooperative learning methods with the Tribes process.

Personalizing the Curriculum

Too many of us in the teaching profession still assume that test scores will go up if **one way or another** we succeed in pouring facts into the heads of students so that they can return it to us either verbally or in written form. Long ago John Dewey (remember him?) urged that educators add a **conceptual level** of teaching which would encourage students to integrate facts into meaningful conceptual thought. Now we are challenged to teach a breed of children who have been conditioned to learn through technology unimagined by our friend John Dewey.

The learning process of children today is very different from that of young people a few decades ago. By the time they enter school the majority have been immersed in countless hours of television which is an experiential medium. It is not a didactic learning medium but **a relational one involving the personal feelings, thoughts and imagination of the viewer**. Like it or not, the learning mode for this generation is stimulated more through an **affective** approach than **cognitive** methods (lectures, questions-answers, memorization).

It is this change in the way our children learn that convinces more schools each year to use experiential and personalized methods in the classroom (ie: learning groups, visual media, role playing, and structured decision-making activities). It gives support to the belief that **we do not have to use traditional teaching methods to teach to traditional tests.**

Students are easily involved in the Tribes process because the many **relational affective activities** engage their personal interests, feelings and imagination. Curricula can come alive by first using inclusion-type activities appealing to the personal feeling level before introducing factual and conceptual information.

One effective way to begin personalizing the lessons is to ask "you-questions" which help the student identify with the subject matter. Here is how you might prepare a lesson on the Columbus story:

1. Review the factual information you want to teach . . .

The Columbus Story

Christopher Columbus was born in Genoa, Italy in the year 1451. Although his father was a weaver, young Christopher wanted to be a sailor. When he was twenty-two years old he went to sea and learned all about charts and maps and navigation. He also heard stories about lands that lay beyond the "Sea of Darkness," as the Atlantic Ocean was called in those days.

People at that time thought that the world was flat, and that if you sailed too far you would fall off the edge. Columbus, however, believed that the world was round, and that if he sailed west, he would eventually reach China and India. He went to many rich and powerful people for money to pay for ships, supplies and crews to make such a voyage. Everyone laughed at him and sent him away.

Finally, with the help of a kindly monk, Columbus was able to persuade Queen Isabella of Spain to finance his voyage. She made him "Admiral of the Ocean Sea" and gave him three ships (named the Nina, the Pinta and the Santa Maria), supplies and able-bodied sailors. They set sail from Spain in August of 1492 and continued for weeks without seeing any sign of land. The crews became frightened and angry and threatened mutiny, but Columbus was able to convince them to go on.

On October 12, 1492, Columbus finally spied land. This turned out to be an island in the Caribbean Sea, which Columbus named San Salvador. He met some dark-skinned natives on this island whom he called Indians, because he believed that he was near the country of India.

Columbus made three more voyages across the Atlantic Ocean, never realizing that he had not reached the Orient, but had discovered an unexplored new land. Eventually, this New World was named America, after Amerigo Vespucci who was another Italian explorer.

2. List the *concepts* and *facts* you want students to learn:

- exploration of an unknown world
- colonialism
- mutiny
- patronage of monarchs to explorers

- flat versus round earth
- role of the sea captain
- dates and names of ships
- name of island
- number of voyages
- Columbus' title

3. Prepare personalized YOU-questions to initiate the lesson:

- Have YOU ever been sailing? How did it feel?
- Did YOU trust the person who was sailing the boat?
- Did you ever have to stand up to a group of people who disagreed with YOU?
- Have YOU ever been to a foreign country where people spoke a different language?
- Did YOU ever have a good idea that no one would accept?

YOU-QUESTIONS ARE:

- Addressed directly to the student;
- Relevant to personal experiences, interests or feelings;
- Meant to evoke personal opinions, preferences, beliefs;
- Intended to help students express hopes, dreams, commitments;
- Shared and discussed with others prior to teaching conceptual-factual curricula.

4. Decide how you will use the questions:

Responses to You-questions are best shared in tribes or smaller sub-groupings of the tribe (dyads or triads). The questions can be used in a writing activity, such as an imaginative letter to a friend or recorded in the student's Personal Journal. Many of the Tribes activities contained in the next chapter can be used to structure sharing responses to YOU-questions. Some suggested ones are:

Open Forum   One-Two-Three
Chain Reaction   Interview Circle
Abstract of Feelings   Daily Community Circle

Let your own imagination go as much as you usually do in your teaching. Your innate ingenuity will invent many creative methods not even mentioned in this book. Just be sure to allow enough time for this important part of the lesson as it stimulates interest and energy for the conceptual and factual levels.

Integrating Cooperative Group Methods with the Tribes Process

It is not the purpose of this book to cover all the excellent cooperative learning methods that are being used throughout the country today. The work of Roger and David Johnson, Robert Slavin, Elliot Aronson, and Gerard Poirier are but a few of the well-evaluated efforts that we urge teachers to draw upon. The Resource Bibliography at the back of this book cites the literature and materials you can obtain to expand your knowledge and repertoire. We do want to give you several methods which are easily used and strengthened by the Tribes process.

The Jigsaw Process[22]

Once the interest of your students has been "captured" on the feeling level, the Jigsaw method is an excellent way to teach subject matter. The technique enables every student to teach other tribe members one part of a lesson. Due to the cohesion and trust that Tribes assures for its members, the process can have great impact on student learning.

Here is how the process works. If you have five tribes, each with a membership of six students, the members count off one-to-six and regroup with students from other tribes. All the number ones are together now, all the twos, the threes, etc. Each jigsaw group is given a part of the class lesson. This could be an arithmetic, social studies, reading, science, current events, health or history lesson such as the Columbus story. For example, if you wished to "jigsaw" the Columbus story, you could give each jigsaw study group one of the paragraphs of the story. It also is important to give study questions to guide the group's work together. Remind them of the Tribe norms and tell them how much time they have to complete their task.

The task of the jigsaw groups is to learn the material and plan how they will present it to the members of their respective tribes. Challenge them to do this creatively, and to include all the factual material and any concepts that they think are important. You can move from group to group to help them with this. The time allotted to learning the material can be anywhere from ten minutes to many days depending upon the complexity of the lesson and age level of the class. When everyone is ready to return to their tribes, ask the people who have the first section to begin. Again, you can move around and lend assistance as needed.

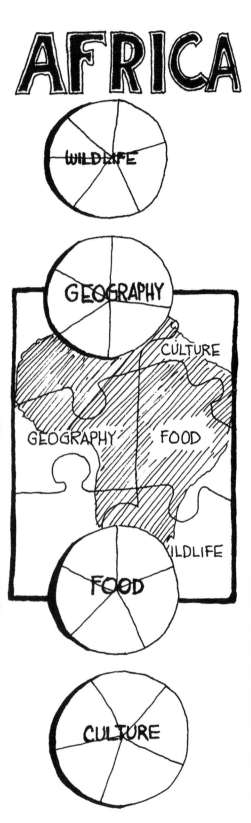

At the conclusion of each presentation or all of the presentations in the tribes, lead a full-group discussion to clarify any part of the lesson. Allow time within each tribe to reflect upon their interaction together and to make statements of appreciation to those who were particularly helpful. Following is a summary of the steps to take in preparing and presenting a Jigsaw lesson.

A Jigsaw Lesson

1. Select a lesson from a curricula unit that you consider appropriate for the process.
2. Divide it into six equal parts (or the number of members per tribe) and define study questions. Prepare sufficient materials for that many study groups.
3. Explain the Jigsaw process to your class. Then ask them to meet in their tribes.
4. If you have not already done so, engage them with an activity on the personal feeling level to awaken interest.
5. Give each tribe one set of lesson material, parts 1–6. Ask each tribe to decide who will be responsible for each part.
6. Ask people responsible for Part 1 to form a jigsaw study group; likewise with parts 2–6.
7. Lead the Jigsaw groups in a brief tribal inclusion activity.
8. Tell the groups what their specific task is and the amount of time that will be allowed. Move from group to group, helping only as needed.
9. When all have finished, ask people to return to their own tribes. If you used lesson dittos, pass out the rest of them to group members so each person has a complete set.
10. Beginning with Part 1, ask students to share the material that they prepared in their Jigsaw group; prepare a format for sharing if you think it will help them when new at this.
11. After each segment has been shared, take time for a full-group discussion and reflecting on the experience.

Discussion: Why was it difficult for Columbus to gain financial backing for his voyage?

Reflection: What was it like to have another student assume the role of teacher? What feelings did you have when you were teaching people in your tribe?

We hasten to acknowledge that at first it may take a little longer to cover a given unit using the Jigsaw process than it might with more traditional methods. The first time around your students will be learning two things at once: the process and the prepared lesson. Be patient and persevering. One of the major benefits to be derived from using this process is the enhancement of each student's self-image (even the slow learners). For a few minutes that student is the "authority," knowing more than the others, on part of the lesson. We are convinced that this "pay-off" in itself more than justifies the extra time that may go into the preparation of a Jigsaw lesson.

The Huddle

So you want something fast and fun that will replace that old question-answer teacher-centered traditional-classroom daily act of yours! You want them just to give you back the facts they should have learned in your lecture or the reading material. And since you have hung in this far with us, you are convinced that it should be a **cooperative** team process. O.K . . . O.K. We hear you.

The Peer Response Huddle

1. Have all tribe members count-off one-to-six (or the number of members per tribe) or pass out numbered cards to each tribe.
2. Ask the class a question, telling the tribes they have 30 seconds to huddle and to decide upon one answer.
3. Instruct the class that when you call out a number, the person in each tribe who has that number will quickly stand up.
4. Ask the first person to stand to give her tribe's answer to the question.
5. Keep the questions, huddle time, calling out numbers and hearing peer responses going as fast as you can so that the energy takes on a "popcorn" effect.

A lot of material can be covered in a brief time. This is an excellent way to do a class review or prepare all students for a test. Once again due to the cooperative group method, more people will know the answers and feel good about themselves.

Tribal Peer Coaching

Now you say you are concerned that some of the poor learners in the class simply are not getting the arithmetic lesson. You have explained something many times. Although most of your students understand the concept, there seem to be some who do not and may need individual attention . . . which you simply do not have the time to give.

Great! How about having peers coach each other! First, we will determine which people in each tribe want to be "coaches" to the less certain students. Coaches are very sure that they understand the lesson that you taught. "Students" are people who would like to have some help. This technique is based on the Client-Consultant activity in Chapter VIII.

Instructions

1. Ask member of your tribes to share which people are very sure that they understand the lesson concept. Ask if those people are willing to be coaches for a brief time to those members who are not as certain.
2. Have people divide up in twos or threes; one student with one or two coaches.
3. Suggest some ways that the coaches can help the students.
4. Tell your coaches that their goal is to have their student be able to repeat back or explain the concept to them.
5. Remind them of their **attentive listening** skills, and tell them how much time they have to work.
6. When the time is up, ask those who were students to explain to their whole tribe what they learned from their coaches.
7. Ask tribes **reflection** questions and give members time to make **statements of appreciation.**

This peer coaching process can also be used just for a few students at times separate from total class involvement (recess, other class lesson time, etc). If you recall one of the research statements earlier in this chapter, you will realize why the process works so well: "Students who feel comfortable with their peers utilize their academic abilities more fully than those who do not."

Designing Lesson Plans

Most of the academic instructional objectives that must be achieved by each class can be easily integrated into the cooperative tribal learning process. Like any other planning that you do for your teaching day, you need to be deliberate about structuring your lesson plan.

Schools are primarily concerned with individual accountability and achievement. As we move to cooperative learning methods, we also need to incorporate methods of accountability for the group's achievement. The correlation between the group's achievement and that of the individuals within effective learning groups is well established. Nevertheless, if possible your lesson plan should include some way to assess the accountability for the task being learned.

On the next page is a cooperative Lesson Plan that can be used to integrate affective and academic objectives, activities and indicators of accountability. The teachers who have been using this form want you to know that they do not detail this completely or in any complex way. It is just for your own use to facilitate planning. Use your own shorthand, language, possible questions and notes so that your adventure with tribal learning groups is a smooth one.

Dear Friends,

I'm a Tribes Program teacher and trainer who has been using the amazing Tribes process in many settings for many years. In schools, the strength of Tribes lies not just in using it now and then for isolated afternoon activities, but as a vehicle to teach curriculum in a positive group setting. Science, math, reading, social science, health and history . . . may all be taught through the Tribes format. The power and strength of the Tribes process appears to me to be directly correlated to the time you as the teacher take to develop adequate **inclusion** in the groups. The stronger that a tribe's sense of inclusion to each other becomes, the more positive their academic learning will be.

As a trainer I often encounter teachers who say they do not always have enough time for Tribes. They feel as the year goes on those special and loved Tribe activities ought to be pushed aside due to the pressures of district mandated testing. The paradox is that the more we can integrate academic material into this supportive process, the better those test scores will be!

Hopefully, the examples in the Activity Section of ways that the Tribes process can be used in teaching curriculum, will set off mental light bulbs expanding your own creative ideas. You are all doing many wonderful activities right now that can be readily adapted to the Tribes format. Remember, nothing really limits us but our own imaginations.

As the late John Lennon said . . ."Imagine!"

Sincerely,

Vicki Stewart

Vicki Stewart
Modesto, California

Materials: **Time Required:**

TRIBES COOPERATIVE LESSON PLAN

Affective Objective:

Academic Objective:

Inclusion Activity:

Cooperative Group Activity:
   (Instruction notes, use of materials,
   time limits, etc.)

Discussion Questions:
   (Configuration: Tribes or Full Class)

Reflection Questions:
   (Configuration: Tribes or Full Class)

To Encourage Appreciation:

Group Accountability:

Individual Accountability:

7

ENGAGING OTHER SYSTEMS
TO SUPPORT DEVELOPMENT

7
Engaging Other Systems To Support Development

T he parking lot next to the school is jam packed because it is "Back-to-School Night." Each fall this event brings more parents out than any other one of the school year. It must be that more realize the importance of their active involvement in their children's schools. As you park your own car between an uppity sports car and an elder station wagon, you feel excited knowing the good energy that hundreds of parents will experience tonight. As the principal of this school, you are proud that last week your "faculty tribes" designed a way for parents to experience the new positive group process being initiated this fall in their children's classrooms. Remarkably enough, hundreds of parents will discuss, prioritize and all in one evening hear a summary of their goals for their children during this school year. Perhaps more important than anything, they will enjoy a time of sharing and support from other parents. "Ha," you muse, "rather different than most parent meetings where people hardly talk to others at all. Perhaps many will want to keep meeting together in "parent tribes.' "

* * * *

Think back a bit to the first chapter of this book. Remember that diagram showing the environmental systems that affect the behavior of each individual? School, family, peers, community, culture, economics all impact each

---

Welcome to
BACK TO SCHOOL NIGHT

Tonight will be a special opportunity for you to experience the kinds of activities that are part of your child's everyday learning in Tribes. It will be a time to talk with other parents like yourselves.

Your Tribe assignment will be in:

Room 22
Teacher: Mrs. Kelley

★★★★★★★★★★★★

young person's development daily. The chart on social development illustrates the key systems which condition behavior and learning for children. There are families, daycare and preschool programs, youth serving agencies and many other childrearing environments that can support and reenforce the social learning initiated in the school. The school itself cannot do it all!

This chapter gives a brief overview of some ways that have been used to extend the Tribes process to other key systems, particularly to parents and with school staffs. Our goal is to have all who influence children's development:

- understand the important roles they play;
- commit to mutually reinforcing the development of positive self-image, social skills and responsibility; and
- strengthen their own respective environmental systems.

Parent Support and Involvement

The inclusive Tribes group process can be used in many creative ways to promote parent support and involvement. Following are but a few examples that Tribe schools have invented and used successfully.

Back-to-School-Night

The vignette at the beginning of this chapter had three objectives to be achieved during visiting night for parents:

- that parents would understand the purposes of the new Tribes Program being used in their children's classrooms;
- that they would enjoy becoming acquainted with other parents, sharing mutual hopes and concerns;
- that having discussed their goals for their own children, they would on that same night in the school auditorium, hear a summary of goals from all of the parents in attendance.

The program design for such an ambitious undertaking follows. The format used here is one that our trainers use to plan and facilitate large meetings or training events.

TIME		ACTIVITY	MATERIALS
7:00	full group	Principal welcomes all & gives, overview of evening program; sends parents to their children's classrooms.	coffee etc.
7:15	tribes	Teacher states hopes for the year, purpose of Tribes program & norms. States that parent class will: experience tribes, discuss and share their goals, prioritize goals of class and go back to auditorium at 9:10 for summary of all parents' goals.	

7:25	tribes	1. Teacher asks all to use norms; facilitates "Name Game" (5 min.)	
		2. Facilitates "I'm Proud" (concerning child or family-10" min)	
7:40	tribes	3. Reflection questions	
7:50	tribes	4. Teacher facilitates "Goal-Storming" (topic: our hope or goals for our child this year) (35 minutes); tribes tally for report back.	newsprint, felt pens, pricing stickers
8:25	full class	5. Parent tribes present their tally of priorities; tribes' top three priorities are recorded on board; all parents then vote for three using marking stickers on board list. Grand tally is made for class report back in auditorium (15 min).	
8:50	full class	6. Teacher leads discussion (emphasize cooperative learning & social development) 7. Reflection questions.	
9:00	tribes	8. Teacher invites statements of appreciation. Parent classes return to auditorium.	handouts
9:10	full group	Principal invites report back of each class' top three priorities. Two parents make tally on large board and total goals to learn parents priorities for year.	
9:25		Principal closes with few remarks. Asks parents to fill out "comment cards" for response to evening.	3" × 5" cards

Parent Support Groups

Parents are people too! We're not sure where that phrase originated, but it seems to be a good one to convey that it isn't all that easy to be a parent in this day and age. The majority of our two-parent families have both parents working; single parent families, now estimated to be more in number than two-parent families, face even more stress. Nevertheless, if we did the exercise cited above with the majority of parents, they would probably be more certain what they wanted for their children than themselves. The question becomes, if an ecological model of development is to be used for children's growth and development, how can the family system be strengthened and supported? How can parents help each other?

The Center for Human Development has three wonderful parent involvement models known as "Parent Educators," "Parent Tribes" and "The Parent Connection." The latter program just grew on its own as parents of a youth drug abuse intervention program (The NEAT Family) realized they had a need to talk with other parents facing difficulties in the adolescent years. Parents themselves take turns facilitating meetings in their homes; they welcome newcomers with warmth and energy, and provide a support that no professional staff could ever equal. Their purpose is to assess the quality of their own family environments, learn skills to maintain open non-judgmental communication with their teenagers, and be there for each other.

The "Parent Tribe Program" is a structured three week series of meetings at a school or community center. Its objectives for attending parents are:

- to improve the confidence of parents in parenting skills;
- to learn ways to support children's development and growth in self-esteem;
- to learn effective communication and problem-solving skills;
- to understand how the development of specific key abilities and attitudes prevents adolescent problems;
- to experience and practice many ways to strengthen the family's quality of time together;
- to explore commonalities and enjoy social support from other parents committed to developing health and capable young people; and
- to have fun!

The sessions use Tribe membership groups, the Tribe norms, group development process and many of the same classroom activities to structure the content for the sessions. The program is facilitated by trained Tribe teachers or administrators. One of the most exciting applications and special refinement of the model came out of a school whose majority population was Cambodian, Spanish-speaking, and Vietnamese. Since so many of the parents only spoke their native language, eight bi-lingual aides were trained to lead the sessions in their respective languages. And not to be outdone, materials were translated into four languages. New American parents are indeed as anxious as others to work together on behalf of their children's growth!

"Parent Educators" is a national award winning model for the prevention of alcohol and drug use among children and youth. Its sophisticated 30 hour training program trains parents themselves to teach drug education curricula in elementary schools. They are trained to integrate curricula into the Tribes process in order to maximize the impact of children's learning, attitudes about drug use and commitment not to use. Thousands of parents in California have been trained and are involved in this impressive volunteer effort. The model, of course, could be used well for any health-oriented content. Evaluations in all schools have been outstanding. Not only does it give parents a new important role in the school, but transfers skills and the developmental process into family settings.

Beyond the many defined programs that evolve out of the Tribes program to reach, support and involve families, school personnel use the principles effectively in relating to parents. What parent conference does not go better if the parent feels rapport (inclusion) with her child's teacher? And what parent group is not impressed when the school itself invites their involvement (inclusion) and influence in the directions the school is taking? The philosophy and skills may be innate with many, but when intentionally applied build a positive climate among any group of people.

Working with Staffs

Let's pause and look at the climate of the staff you may may be working on? How many of the following questions can you respond to positively?

- I can go to more than two other people at any time and ask for assistance without embarrassment or apology. Yes/No?
- Our staff meetings are interesting, productive and supportive. Yes/No?
- The principal or administrator involves staff in appropriate decisions. Yes/No?
- My suggestions, innovations and ideas are heard and welcomed. Yes/No?
- The environment of our staff as a system is positive and caring? Yes/No?

Now don't quit yet! Your staff is not the only one who wonders if there isn't a better way.

In order to create a supportive learning environment for children, the staff itself needs to be experiencing a similar support environment. Social support alleviates stress. Both stress reduction and effective classroom environments can be assured whenever a school commits to using "faculty tribes" or staff support groups.

To do this, the principal or administrator must be willing to decentralize some of the decision-making and encourage collegial support among the faculty. The pay-off is that his job will be much easier and faculty morale improved 100%.

Many Tribe schools have learned this as they converted the classroom model to staff use. Teachers can divide up into membership groupings (long-term tribes) either by grade levels, buildings/pods, at random or interest areas. The tribes meet often, and are used within the faculty meeting for discussion, planning, brainstorming, prioritizing and mutual support. The now familiar process of inclusion, influence and affection creates a new positive working environment.

One of the greatest innovations that one school started was to invite any teacher who just wanted to talk about a concern to post a sign in the faculty room. The sign would say something like "I need two or three 'consultants' at 3 o'clock today. Will be here waiting." Using the format of the "Client-Consultant Activity" of this book, staff members help each other clarify concerns about children, curricula or various behavioral problems. The principals of schools who use this method report that their office has fewer discipline problems to handle. Several heads and hearts are always better than one going it alone!

Childcare Programs

With the ever-growing majority of parents working and having to leave their children in childcare facilities, many now seek more than just "custodial" care. Young parents are realizing that the quality of the pre-school or after-school care is critical in supporting their children's learning and development. The important "3 R's" which we call Relatedness, Respect and

Responsibility begins at birth. Who has not recognized the spark in infants' eyes as they respond to the smiles, touch, encouragement and voices of parents and other caretakers? These moments of warmth and relatedness build self-esteem. When a child is deprived of such care, they are less likely to be curious, to love learning and to enjoy others. Our childrearing systems have the opportunity and responsibility to further the social development of children. The exciting news is that many pre-school and after-school daycare programs within community and school settings are now using the Tribes process to do so.

The process gives them a way to structure the childcare environment so that it is more supportive and positive just as tribal classrooms are. Very small children, ages two and three, feel more secure when they are paired into groups of three or four and given a permanent space of their own in a room. Behavior problems lessen and all begin to learn to help care for each other. Cooperative activities rather than individual ones are used; and the norms of listening, right to pass and no put downs but appreciation are easily adopted.

The plight of after-school daycare needing to keep older children busy several hours per day is also transformed when the Tribes process is used. Planning can be decentralized to membership groups of the children, leadership is encouraged, and the usual negative climate is replaced with a positive one. Cooperative interaction activities from this book and others are used to structure the hours of play or crafts. Again, the environment produced from the Tribe norms makes all the difference in children's behavior and time together.

Daycare programs that have as their focus the development of pro-social behaviors among children are really doing **prevention**. As pointed out earlier in Chapter 1, anti-social behaviors in young children clearly predict problems in the adolescent and adult years. And low self-esteem is predictive of later struggles in academic achievement. We are convinced that childcare programs and centers can make a big difference in human development.

Center Source Publications will release a book on these important childcare applications during the coming year.

8

TRIBAL ACTIVITIES

8 Tribal Activities

Now and then throughout the years that the Tribes Program has been in existence, a statement such as the following makes its way back to us: "I bought a copy of the Tribes book to use the activities in my class, but I was really disappointed! The curriculum didn't seem to work very well with my students." Of course not!

The Tribes Program is a process. It is not a glossy set of "content-validated-lesson-plans arranged in prescribed-curriculum-units." Tribes is a **process**, and as we've said many times before, the **activities alone are not enough!**

A process is a flowing experience, a journey composed of a sequential series of events that culminate in the achievement of a goal. Activities are some of those events, but as you know by now the tribes process evolves out of the important moments happening between people. The positive groundrules, caring communication and cooperative spirit of the program create the journey. To use the activities alone without intentionally developing the supportive process is like paddling a canoe in a dry creek.

It is the activities that provide a format or the structure for subject matter, personal learning or skill development content. **They must be tailored to fit the ethnicity, socio-economic culture, age level, interests and language of the students in your class.** Adapting activities to suit the ethnicity and culture of a group is challenging. First, one must appreciate the uniqueness of customs, attitudes and behaviors that the population normally practices. An activity that is not adapted or modified may antagonize people and set back the process. Examples:

- Using the names of Christian holidays but not those of other religions;
- Asking people of collective traditions (Asian, American Indian and some Hispanic) to make personal statements during the inclusion stage when the opportunity first to present information about their culture, family or group is more traditional and comfortable;
- Ignoring the economic realities of a community (ie: using examples of luxury items in low-income area);

- Admonishing some Asian group members during a listening activity to maintain eye contact (when in their own culture averting one's eyes denotes respect);
- Using examples of or expecting higher levels of self-actualization (intimacy, creativity) in a group that still may be concerned with basic security. Or the opposite: security level content for a group seeking creativity.

Consideration must also be given to the existing stage of the group's development so that the activity meets the needs of group members. The activities of this chapter are arranged in the stages in which the tribes process evolves. The first set promote **inclusion** and those which appear later facilitate the **influence** stage. There also is a section which gives examples for teaching **subject matter** and a collection of our favorite **energizers** to spark classroom fun and community spirit.

Notations on each activity will tell you:

1. Suggested grade levels
2. Group configuration (full group, sub-group or Tribe)
3. Approximate time required
4. Materials needed
5. Subject matter (if appropriate)

Also included for each activity are:

Objectives
Instructions
Discussion and Reflection Questions
Appreciation Statements

REMEMBER: THE ACTIVITY ALONE IS NOT ENOUGH

Each shared tribe or group experience needs to be followed by Discussion, Reflection and statements of Appreciation providing opportunities for insight, self-awareness and learning. The follow-up after each activity, the supportive norms and the intentional group development process are all essential components. Combined they add up to the **power** of the tribes process.

The tribal activities in this book are meant to be suggestions only to stimulate your thinking so that you can modify or invent the most appropriate ones for your class. Remember the importance of the teacher-facilitator's personal awareness during the activity so that meaningful discussion, reflection and appreciation statements can be created. In time you will realize as hundreds of other tribe teachers have that you will never "run out" of activities once you experience and internalize the Tribes Program's creative teaching process.

There are no hard and fast rules . . . experiment!

Tribal Activity Log

An activity log can provide you with a quick and easy way to keep track of all the activities that you introduce to your class, and how your students respond. It gives you an on-going picture of how the process is unfolding with your tribes, and it will also:

- Let you know which types of activities are most effective;
- Provide information you can share with other tribes teachers when you meet together for planning and support;
- Provide a "self-critique" that will help you improve your facilitation skills;
- Help you to determine where you are in terms of inclusion, influence or affection stages. This in turn enables you to select activities that are appropriate for the group stage that your class is experiencing.

Credit, Applause and an Invitation

Many of these activities have been adapted from other sources, some familiar to you. The Resource Section following this chapter contains listings of many collections. Some of the best, however, have been contributed by creative Tribe teachers. We hope that you will send us all the great ones that you come up with for the next edition of this book; we would like to buy them from you if they are written up in our format. Activities, like the rest of this book will always be in a process of revision as we all learn more about this exciting educational journey that we are on together.

Keep in mind, YOU are the only one who can properly adapt, translate or create the most appropriate activity models for your class. Your own sensitivity as a teacher is the most important resource for your students.

So have fun, and . . . Trust the Process!

Daily Community Circle Activity

Grades: K-3
Time: 20 minutes
Grouping: full
Materials: none

Objectives

1. To build inclusion
2. To learn what is happening with the total group
3. To accomplish housekeeping and administrative needs
4. To teach effective communication skills

Setting The Scene. On the first day of school state to the children and all others that are part of the classroom family (aides, parents, student teachers, etc.) that first thing every morning we will meet in a Community Circle. Explain that we sit in a circle because we can all see and hear each other best that way. Describe the norms that are to be followed: Active Listening, Right to Pass, and No Put downs.

Instructions

1. Meet in Community Circle.
2. Take care of administrative and housekeeping needs such as attendance, notices and clean up assignments.
3. Review "schedule-of-the-day" so that each child knows the curriculum groupings, projects and tribes activities planned for the day.
4. Review the norms.
5. Ask a "question-of-the-day" (e.g., I feel happy when . . .). See suggested examples listed on the next page.
6. Have children respond in turn to the question. Allow time at the end for those children who passed to respond if they desire.

Discussion

Ask questions such as:
- What are some things that make us happy?
- Did you hear anything new?
  What were some similarities/differences?

Reflection

Ask questions such as:
- Was it hard for you to think of something to say?
- How did you feel sharing yourself in this group?

Appreciation

Suggest people make statements of appreciation:
- "I liked it when . . ."
- "I feel like you when . . ."

Suggested Questions-of-the-Day

1. I feel happy when . . .
2. I feel sad when . . .
3. I feel angry when . . .
4. I feel scared when . . .
5. The scariest thing is . . .
6. The biggest thing in the world . . .
7. I'm bigger than . . .
8. I'm smaller than . . .
9. The smallest thing is . . .
10. My favorite toy is . . .
11. My favorite pet is . . .
12. My favorite food is . . .
13. My favorite T.V. show is . . .
14. My favorite song is . . .
15. My favorite story is . . .
16. My favorite color is . . .
17. My favorite weather is . . .
18. Rain makes me feel . . .
19. Wind makes me feel . . .
20. Sunshine makes me feel . . .
21. Snow makes me feel . . .
22. Fog makes me feel . . .
23. When I think of blue I think of . . .
24. When I think of red I think of . . .
25. When I think of green I think of . . .
26. When I think of yellow I think of . . .
27. When I think of orange I think of . . .
28. When I think of black I think of . . .
29. When I think of brown I think of . . .
30. Today I feel . . .
31. What Is something scratchy . . .
32. What is something soft . . .
33. What is something sharp . . .
34. What is something smooth . . .
35. What is something sour . . .
36. What is something sweet . . .
37. What is something cold . . .
38. What is something cool . . .
39. What is something warm . . .
40. What is something how . . .
41. If I were an animal, I would be . . .
42. If I were a building, I would be a . . .
43. The first thing I want to do when I grow up is . . .
44. When I grow up, I want to be . . .

Note: The best questions are those most relevant to the children's experiences.

Me Book

Grades: K-3
Time: 20 minutes/day, 10 consecutive days
Grouping: full, tribe
Materials: construction paper, pencils, felt pens, crayons

Objectives

1. To build self-esteem and self-awareness
2. To reinforce relationship between oral and written language
3. To experience working on a long range project

Instructions

1. The teacher explains to the full group that each student will be making a "Me Book." Each day for ten consecutive school days, the teacher gives a statement that each child completes.

   Sample statements:
   - I feel great when . . .
   - I feel angry when . . .
   - I feel sleepy when . . .
   - My Mom thinks I'm . . .
   - My Dad thinks I'm . . .
   - I feel my brother is . . .
   - I feel my sister is . . .
   - My favorite toy is . . .
   - My favorite food is . . .
   - The place I like best to be is . . .

   Note: For very young children, have them dictate to aide or an older student.
2. Have students form tribes and draw a picture that answers the statement.
3. Use adult aides or cross-age tutors to facilitate. Ask: How could you draw yourself feeling good? What do you do with your hands when you're mad?
4. After each page is drawn, have aide or student write the child's explanation of the drawing.

Discussion

Ask questions like:
- Who would like to share part of their "Me Book?"
- What is your favorite food? Favorite toy?

Reflection

- Was it hard to think of things to draw?
- Did you discover anything about yourself?

Appreciation

Suggest people make statements of appreciation:
- "What I like about your "Me Book" is . . .
- "I liked it when . . ."

Objectives

1. To demonstrate the power of non-verbal communication
2. To promote cooperation and fun
3. To build inclusion and influence

Instructions

1. Form dyads (pair off in twos).
2. Each dyad is given one crayon and one piece of construction paper.
3. Partners may not talk to each other or decide prior to activity which picture they will draw as a team.
4. While a 3 or 4 minute song is played in the background, both partners hold crayon simultaneously and non-verbally draw any picture together.

Discussion

Ask questions such as:
- What did you draw? What does it represent?
- What have we learned about sharing and cooperation?

Reflection

Ask questions such as:
- Was it difficult not to talk to your partner?
- Did each partner share equally in the making of the picture?
- Which partner was the leader? How did you know?
- How did you feel when you realized your picture was going to be something?

Appreciation

Suggest people make statements of appreciation:
- "I liked it when . . ."
- "I felt good when . . ."
- "I like your picture because . . ."

Two On A Crayon

Grades: K-3
Time: 20 minutes
Grouping: dyads
Materials: paper, crayons, music

Now I Am

Grades: K-3
Time: 20 minutes
Grouping: full
Materials: none

Objectives

1. To recognize and identify feelings
2. To introduce relationship between oral and written language
3. To develop observation skills

Instructions

1. Sit in full-group circle; observe norms.
2. Whisper specific feeling or emotion in each student's ear one at a time:

fear	frustration	surprise	rage
upset	hope	soreness	love
dreaming	tired	anger	wild
unhappiness	uncomfortable	embarrassed	weird
itchy	stubborn	excitement	sleepy
nervous			

3. After student hears feeling word, he/she acts out word non-verbally (some may be repeated).
4. The whole community guesses what is being acted out.

Discussion

Ask questions such as:
- Was it hard to "act out" a feeling?
- How did you figure out what feelings were being represented?

Reflection

- Which of these feelings have you experienced?
- Would anyone like to share a time when he/she felt one of these feelings?

Appreciation

Suggest people make statements of appreciation:
- "I liked the way you acted it out because . . ."
- "I feel a lot like you when . . ."

Follow-Up Activities:

1. Draw feelings using colors that match the feeling.
2. Make a face of how you feel this minute
3. Write a story about a person always acting the same
4. Print feeling words on cards, and have people do them.

Objectives

1. To build inclusion
2. To encourage sharing

Instructions

1. Members are seated in a circle.
2. Each participant takes a turn at answering the question: "What kind of animal do you feel like today?"

Discussion

Ask questions such as:
- Would someone like to tell what animals were in his or her Tribe today?
- Were there any similar animals mentioned?

Reflection

Ask questions such as:
- Was it hard to think of the right animal?
- When was the last time you felt like this animal?

Appreciation

Suggest people make statements of appreciation:
- "I liked your animal because . . ."
- "I'm like your animal when . . ."

Zoo Stories

Grades: K-3
Time: 20 minutes
Grouping: tribe
Materials: none

What Feelings Do You Have?

Grades: K-3
Time: 30 minutes
Grouping: full
Materials: chalkboard, chalk, chart, paper, pens

Objectives

1. To build inclusion
2. To encourage participants to talk about their feelings

Instructions

1. Begin exercise as full group discussion of feelings
2. Chart the discussion results as follows:

Feeling:	Three colors which seem to fit the feeling:
1. Happy	Yellow, Pink, Orange
2. Angry	Black, Red, Brown
3. Sad	Blue, White, Black

Discussion

Ask questions such as:

- What different kinds of feelings do you have?
- Do our feelings change from time to time?
- What makes you angry/happy/sad?

Reflection

Ask questions such as:

- "I'm a lot like you when . . ."
- "I admired your honesty about . . ."

Objectives

1. To build inclusion
2. To express feelings in the colors

Instructions

1. Ask participants to form groups of 4 to 6 or meet in tribes.
2. Give each participant a piece of art paper and brush.
3. Have group choose three colors; place colors on lid for each child.
4. Instruct each member to paint a picture, using the colors, which represents how he/she is feeling (refer to chart made in previous activity, What Feelings Do You Have).
5. Have each member share the feeling he/she painted with the group.

Discussion

Ask questions such as:

- What were the different feelings painted in the group?
- How did you decide which feeling to paint?

Reflection

Ask questions such as:

- How did you feel while painting?
- How do you feel right now?

Appreciation

Suggest people make statements of appreciation:

- "I'm a lot like you when . . ."
- "I admired your honesty about . . ."
- "I liked it when you . . ."

Abstract Painting of Feelings

Grades: K-3
Time: 30 minutes
Grouping: tribe or sub-group
Materials: 12″ × 18″ paper, paints, brushes, lids, water

Silhouettes

Grades: K-3
Time: 1 hour or more
Grouping: dyads
Materials: construction paper, pencils, scissors, glue, magazines

Objectives

1. To build self-esteem
2. To promote inclusion
3. To encourage positive statements towards one another

Instructions

1. Have participants form dyads.
2. Instruct dyads to place construction paper on wall. Darken room and place a bright light close to a wall.
3. Have one person sit between light and wall, making a profile shadow on paper.
4. Tell the partner to outline the shadow with a pencil.
5. After both silhouettes have been traced, ask each participant to cut out and mount the silhouette.
6. Have each participant select magazine pictures which represent how he/she feels about himself/herself.
7. Display silhouettes on bulletin board. Under each place an envelope with the name of student drawn in big letters.
8. Explain that the envelopes are for written "warm fuzzy" statements which will be placed in envelopes during the year.
9. Ask students to draw names and place a written "warm fuzzy" in appropriate envelope. Writers are to remain anonymous.

Discussion

Ask questions such as:
- Were there similarities/differences in the pictures we used to represent how we feel?
- What are some of the things you like to do?

Reflection

Ask questions such as:
- How did you feel when you saw your "warm fuzzy"?
- How did you feel when you were looking for pictures to represent yourself?

Appreciation

Suggest people make statements of appreciation:
- "I liked it when . . ."
- "I am a lot like you because . . ."

Mirror . . . Mirror

Grades: K-3
Time: 45 minutes
Grouping: full or tribe
Materials: a hand mirror, hand mirror worksheets, crayons

Objectives

1. To provide an opportunity for people to present themselves to each other
2. To facilitate sharing feelings
3. To build acceptance for individual diversity, ethnicity and culture
3. To teach "I-Messages"
4. To build inclusion

Instructions

1. Invite all people to stand in one large circle, and pass around a hand mirror.
2. Lead a discussion that points out that mirrors reflect how people all look different in special ways (color or hair, eyes, skin, smiles etc); but that mirrors do not show what people think and feel which is also very important.
3. Pass out mirror worksheets and ask people to divide into tribes to complete the worksheet pictures of themselves. Have aides or older children help the non-readers if necessary.
4. Have the children share their mirrors either in tribes or the full group.

Discussion

- What did you learn about someone else you didn't know before?
- What differences and similarities were in your mirrors?

Reflection

- How did you feel sharing your mirror?
- Did you feel people were listening when you took your turn
- Do you feel proud about who you are?

Appreciation

"I liked it when . . ."
"I liked Joel's mirror because . . ."
"I think you are neat because . . ."

Tribe Program Handout

Mirror-Mirror

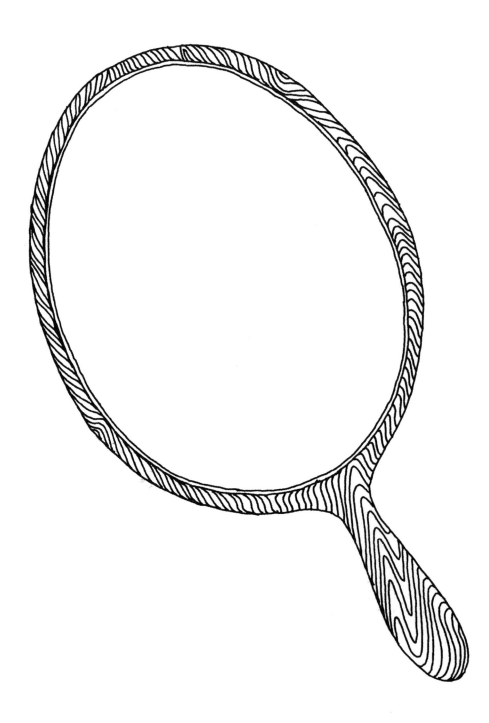

Objectives

1. To build inclusion
2. To encourage verbal ability especially with ESL (english as a second language) children
3. To express likes and dislikes, and promote acceptance of individual diversity
4. To learn shapes (circle and triangle)

Instructions

1. Have children stand in large circle, and ask them to take turn stating their favorite color.
2. Tell them to huddle with two other people and tell each other what their favorite toy may be; huddle again with two other different people and tell them what their favorite food is. For grades 2-3, have them huddle one more time with two others to share something that they dislike.
3. Have everyone come back to the full circle and join hands; sing or recite rhyme below:
   "I like you . . . I like me
   Special people one, two, three,
   Different colors . . . different eyes
   Each of us is quite a prize!"
   (Lead a big cheer after this.)
4. Have people get into groups of three within their tribes
5. Pass out circle-triangle worksheets; tell children to draw:
   • under one side of triangle favorite color
   • under one side: favorite toy
   • under one side: favorite food
6. Then tell them to draw a picture (in the middle of the triangle) of a person they really admire or like. We urge you to vary the content from what is suggested above. It needs to be appropriate to their age level and culture.
7. Children can share one or all sections of their circle-triangles with their tribes or the full classroom.

Discussion

   • Was this a good activity?
   • How are a lot of people alike? How are they different?

Reflection

   • Do you feel special about who you are? Are you proud?
   • Was this fun?

Appreciation

   • "I like you because . . ."
   • "I liked it when . . ."

My Favorite People and Things

Grades: K-3
Time: 30 minutes
Grouping: triads within tribes
Materials: circle/triangle worksheets, pencils, crayons

Tribes Program Handout

My Favorite People and Things

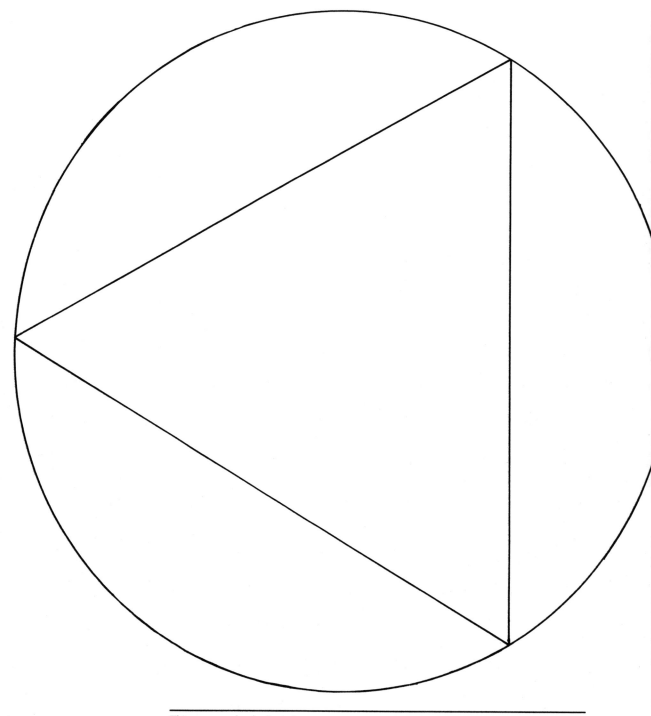

Objectives

1. To build community inclusion
2. To divide people into tribe groups
3. To have a hilarious time

Instructions

1. In order to divide people into tribe groups, prepare small slips of paper for each person. Depending on the number of groups that people will divide into, choose the names of that many noisy animals. Examples: horse, cow, chicken, pig, sheep, donkey.
2. Write the names of the animals on the slips so that the number of people you want in the "horse" tribe all have a slip labeled "horse"; and the number for the "chicken" tribe all have a slip marked "chicken."
3. If you are designating specific people for membership in each tribe, write their names on the outside of their respective slips with the proper animal tribe name inside.
4. Before distributing the slips, tell everyone that they are not to let anyone else know what their slip says.
5. When all are ready, have the community circulate around with eyes closed, making the noise of their animal until they find all the other same animals.
6. After all have found their groups, have them sit together to discuss and reflect upon the experience.

Discussion

- What do you think of this method of building tribes?
- What do you imagine the neighbors think is happening in here?

Reflection

- How did you feel wandering around seeking your animal friends?
- What was it like finding the first one?
- How did your group stay together?
- Look at each other now. How do you feel?

Appreciation

- "I was . . . when . . ."
- "Thank you, . . . for . . ."
- "I liked it when . . ."

Barnyard Babble

Grades: K-adult
Time: 15 minutes
Grouping: full
Materials: name slips

Joy

Grades: 2-adult
Time: 20 minutes
Grouping: full group or tribe
Materials: none

Objectives

1. To give each person an opportunity to share something special or personal with others
2. To increase communication skills
3. To build inclusion

Instruction.

1. Ask each person to think of three things that he/she would like to share. Use the first letters of the word "joy" to structure what is to be shared:

   J: something in your life that **just** happened
   O: **one** thing you would like to do for yourself
   Y: a part of **you** that makes you a very special person

   You might want to point out that the key (underlined) words for the sentences say, "just one you!"
2. Urge people to listen attentively as each speaker takes a turn sharing.

Discussion

- Was this a good activity to help people learn more about each other?
- Do people often begin a meeting or party this way? Why not?

Reflection

- How did you feel while you were speaking to the group?
- Did you feel people were listening well? How could you tell?
- When was the last time that you experienced sharing this much of you to others?
- How does the group feel now?

Appreciation

Invite statements of appreciation
- "It helped me when . . ."
- "I appreciated . . ."
- "Thank you for . . ."

Objectives

1. To explore individual attitudes about the use of alcohol or drugs
2. To practice attentive listening skills
3. To build peer support

Instructions

1. Have people divide up into dyads, and decide whether they will be an "A" or a "B." Pass out pre-prepared question slips which are on the following page, or generate appropriate questions for the culture and age level of your own students.
2. Suggest that all of the pairs move to a comfortable place where they can hear each other well. Tell them that A is to begin answering the questions while B listens, and that at the end of five minutes you will signal for them to rotate roles. Remind them of the norms, particularly attentive listening.
3. Give the signal to rotate after five minutes, and call the dyads back to the full group after the additional five minutes.
4. Discuss and reflect on the experience in the full group.

Discussion

- How many people learned something about drugs or themselves? What was it?
- Is an activity like this sharing with a peer supportive so that people are comfortable talking?

Reflection

- Were you more comfortable talking or listening?
- Did you feel your partner really cared about what you were saying?
- When was the last time that you ever talked about alcohol or drug use? Is it helpful?

Appreciation

- "I really appreciated it when . . ."
- ". . . , you are special because . . ."
- "Thank you, . . ."

Taking a Closer Look

Grades: 5-adult
Time: 30 minutes
Grouping: subgroups in tribes
Materials: question slips

Question Slip

Taking a Closer Look

1. What kinds of messages did you get about alcohol or drugs when you were younger (right or wrong to use? O.K. for men, not women? Beer and wine don't hurt you?)

2. Where did these messages come from? (School, family, media, church, friends?)

3. What was the first decision you ever made about choosing to use or not use alcohol or drugs? How old were you? What happened? What process did you use to make a decision?

4. Describe what your life would be like if you did not use alcohol and/or drugs? (Option: what it might be like if you did use? Ask non-users about over-the-counter or prescription drugs they may use. Coffee?)

5. What would you want your brother, sister or child to know that you have learned about chemical substances?

6. Would you feel comfortable with your child using drugs or alcohol as much as you do?

Pantomime

Grades: K-3
Time: 20 minutes
Grouping: full
Materials: none

Objectives

1. To build self-esteem
2. To build inclusion
3. To experience communication without words

Instructions

1. Form two groups with one group sitting inside circle and the other group outside circle.
2. Each group has a turn doing expressions and movement.
3. There is no discussion until both groups have finished exercise.
4. The following are suggestions of expressions and movement:
   • facial expressions: funny faces, feel scared, feel sad
   • feeling walks: walk angrily, walk sadly
   • weather walks: walk in the rain
   • people walks: robber, clown
   • animal walks: dog, cat, duck
   • characters and situations: an acrobat on a tightrope
   • exploring senses: taste a lemon, smell a skunk
   • handling imaginary objects: play with a yo-yo
   • experiencing different environments: you are on the moon

Discussion

Ask questions such as:
   • When was the last time you felt happy/sad/angry/etc.?

Reflection

Ask questions such as:
   • Did you feel others watched and listened? How did you know?
   • How did you feel while participating in the exercise?

Appreciation

Suggest people make statements of appreciation:
   • "I liked it when . . ."
   • "I'm like you when . . ."
   • "I felt good when . . ."

Gallery Walks

Grades: K-3
Time: 30 minutes
Grouping: full
Materials: student art work

Objectives

1. To build communication skills
2. To build self-esteem and pride in work
3. To build inclusion and influence

Instructions

1. Several participants are assigned the roles of "curators"; and the remaining people form triads.
2. Triads take a "gallery walk" around room to view articles on display, projects-in-making, etc.
3. Student-curators stand by their Masterpieces and share with viewers the origin of their ideas, materials used, personal objectives incorporated into task, feelings about finished work, etc.

Discussion

Ask questions such as:
- What kinds of things did the curators mention most?
- Can we note similarities and differences among the curators? People in general?
- What have we learned about the variety of talent in our class?

Reflection

Ask questions:
- How did you feel about sharing your Masterpiece?
- Did the group listen? How did you know?
- Was it easier to explain your work to the 2nd, 3rd and then 4th group (indicating more self-confidence)?
- How did the curators seem to feel about their work?

Appreciation

Suggest people make statements of appreciation:
- "I liked it when you said . . ."
- "Some of your talents are . . ."
- "I like your Masterpiece because . . ."

Creative Storytelling

Grades: K-6
Time: 15-30 minutes
Grouping: full
Materials: none

Objectives

1. To encourage listening
2. To promote free expression of fantasy
3. To develop group cohesion

Instructions

1. Tell people, "we are going to make up a group story together."
2. Give instructions as follows: "The leader will start by saying a few sentences, then we'll choose someone to continue story where the first person left off. That person will do the same until the story goes around the circle two or three times.
3. Choose a setting for the story which involves children themselves, yet leaves lots of room for fantasizing. Example: "Once there were a group of kids named _____, _____, _____, and _____, who wanted to find a place to go swimming together. They came upon a big water hole which looked very inviting. But as soon as one jumped in, a funny animal reared its head from out of the water. . . ."
4. Encourage children to listen to each other and to continue the story in whatever way they want to.
5. Mention the "right to pass."

Discussion

Ask the questions such as:
- What do you think of our story?
- How would it have been different if just one person had told the story?

Reflection

- What feelings did you have during the story?
- Which did you enjoy more, telling your part of the story or listening to others?

Appreciation

Suggest people make statements of appreciation:
- "I like your part of the story because . . ."
- "I felt good when . . ."

Fuzzyland Map

Grades: K-5
Time: 40 Minutes
Grouping: tribe, sub-group
Materials: large sheets of paper (24″ × 36″). colored markers, crayons.

Objectives

1. To give opportunity for presentation of self to tribe
2. To build tribe inclusion through involvement in a task
3. To facilitate cooperative tribe norms
4. To facilitate the giving and accepting of appreciation statements

Instructions

1. Plan to do this activity early in the day, possibly just 40 minutes before recess.
2. Ask class to meet in tribes; proceed with instructions as soon as people are seated quietly.
3. If your class is somewhat "sophisticated" (as is often the case with grades 4–6), you may explain that the story you are about to tell is one which they can relate to their younger brothers and sisters, to help them understand about getting along with people and making friends.
4. Ask the class, if they wish, to close their eyes and visualize the story as you tell it, but to remain silent until the story is over.
5. Read (or preferably, tell) the story "Fuzzyland."
6. Discuss and clarify the meaning of the story. Ask questions such as:
   • What is a Warm Fuzzy? a Cold Prickly?
   • Why, in the story, did people need Warm Fuzzies?
   • Why did people stop giving Warm Fuzzies freely after the witch cast her spell?
7. Give each tribe a large sheet of paper and colored markers or crayons.
8. Review the norms. Ask the members of each tribe together to create a map of Fuzzyland. Encourage each person to draw some part of his map. Tell them they will have fifteen minutes to do this, and that you will let them know when only five minutes remain.
9. Visit each tribe to make sure the instructions are clear.
10. Stand back and observe tribes as they work together. Help those that seem to have problems.
11. When time is up, ask each tribe to appoint a spokesperson to share their map with the full group. Encourage other members to share what they have contributed.

Discussion

Facilitate dialogue among tribes by asking questions such as:
   • What similarities are there among your Fuzzyland maps? Differences?
   • What colors did you use to represent the different characters and places in the story?
   • For older children: How did you approach the task, make decisions, assign roles, as a tribe?
   • How could we use these maps to help younger children understand about Warm Fuzzies and Cold Pricklies? Encourage tribe members to talk to one another rather than to you.

Reflection

Ask questions such as:
- Were the norms observed as you worked together?
- To what extent did all the tribe members participate in the activity?
- Which part of the story did you have the strongest feelings about?
- How can we make this class more like Fuzzyland?

Appreciation

Ask each tribe member to give someone in the tribe a "Warm Fuzzy," such as:
- "I liked it when you said . . ."
- "You're neat because . . ."
- "I'm like you when . . ."

Fuzzyland*

Once upon a time, a long time ago and far from here, there was a place called Fuzzyland. People were very happy in Fuzzyland because in those happy times everyone at birth was given a small soft, Fuzzy Bag. Any time a person reached into this bag he was able to pull out a Warm Fuzzy. Warm Fuzzies were very much in demand because whenever somebody was given a Warm Fuzzy, it made him feel warm and good all over. People who didn't get Warm Fuzzies regularly were in danger of developing a sickness called "Fuzzy Deficiency Anemia." Their backs would shrivel up, and they would shrink up so much in size that they would hide from people.

In those days it was very easy to get Warm Fuzzies. Anytime you wanted a Warm Fuzzy, all you had to do was walk up to someone and say, "I'd like a Warm Fuzzy, please." The person would then reach into his bag and pull out a Fuzzy the size of a little girl's hand. As soon as the Fuzzy saw the light of day, it would smile and blossom into a large, shaggy Warm Fuzzy. The person would then lay it on your shoulder or head or lap and it would snuggle up and melt against your skin and make you feel good all over. You could give yourself a Warm Fuzzy, but it always seemed to feel nicer if someone else gave you one. So, fuzzies were always given freely and getting enough of them was never a problem. Fuzzyland was a happy place because everyone felt so friendly and good most of the time.

One day a bad witch came to Fuzzyland and tried to sell people her strange potions and salves. When no one wanted to buy them (because they all felt so good) she became very angry and cast an evil magic spell on the people of Fuzzyland. The spell made them believe that Warm Fuzzies were getting scarce, that eventually they would run out, and there wouldn't be any left. So people reached in less and less into their Fuzzybags and became very stingy. Everyone began to notice the lack of Warm Fuzzies and newspapers carried stories about the "great fuzzy shortage." People started to feel that they were shrinking, so they went to the witch to buy her potions and salves, even though they didn't seem to keep anyone's back from shriveling up.

The bad witch didn't really want people to shrink and hide (who then would buy things from her?). So she devised a new scheme. She gave everyone a bag that was very similar to a Fuzzy Bag, except this one was cold instead of warm. Inside the bags that the witch gave people were Cold Pricklies. These Cold Pricklies did not make people feel warm and fuzzy, but made them feel cold, prickly and crabby instead. From then on, people who would not share Warm Fuzzies would give away Cold Prickles.

So although there were not that many people shrinking and hiding yet, a lot of people were unhappy feeling very cold, prickly and crabby. The situation in Fuzzyland had become very, very sad. Remember, it really all began with the coming of the bad witch who made people believe that there was beginning to be a shortage of Warm Fuzzies in their land.

Finally, on one sunny day a good witch arrived in Fuzzyland. She had not heard about the bad witch and was not affected by the evil magic spell. She wasn't worried about running out of Warm Fuzzies at all, but gave them away freely even when not asked. She was a kind witch and knew Cold Prickly's were bad for people. She never ever would give anyone a Cold Prickly. Many people disapproved of her because she was giving children the idea that they really should never worry about running out of Warm Fuzzies. And then a new wonderful magic began to happen! Each time the good witch gave a child one of her Warm Fuzzies, the bad witch's evil spell was broken, and that child could in turn break the evil spell again by giving someone else a Warm Fuzzy. Many people, children and grown ups alike, were so used to exchanging Cold Pricklies that at first they refused to accept Warm Fuzzies. But the children whom the good witch had befriended kept giving Warm Fuzzies freely until everyone in Fuzzyland was once again feeling good and warm and fuzzy all over . . . everyone, that is, except the bad witch. They say that she just sneaked out of Fuzzyland one dark night hoping to peddle her potions and salves elsewhere.

*This story has been adapted from *A Fairy Tale* by Claude Steiner, Sacramento, CA: JALMAR Press, Inc. 1977. Mr. Steiner has given permission for the adaptation and its use in this book.

Warm Fuzzies

Grades: K-5
Time: 30 minutes
Grouping: tribes
Materials: left over yardage, yarn, netting, trim, fringe, glue, scissors, pencils.

Objectives

1. To build inclusion
2. To encourage expression of positive feelings towards others

Instructions

1. Ask participants to meet in tribes.
2. Instruct each participant to create a warm fuzzy from the available materials. Children (grades 2-5) may enjoy making warm fuzzy "pom-poms." Instructions are included on the next page. Younger children may need assistance.

Discussion

Ask such questions as:
- What is a warm fuzzy?
- Why did you pick the material that you did?

Reflection

Ask questions such as:
- How did you feel while you were creating your warm fuzzy?

Appreciation

Suggest people make statements of appreciation:
- "I like the warm fuzzy you made because . . ."
- "I feel good when . . ."

Instructions for Making a Warm Fuzzy

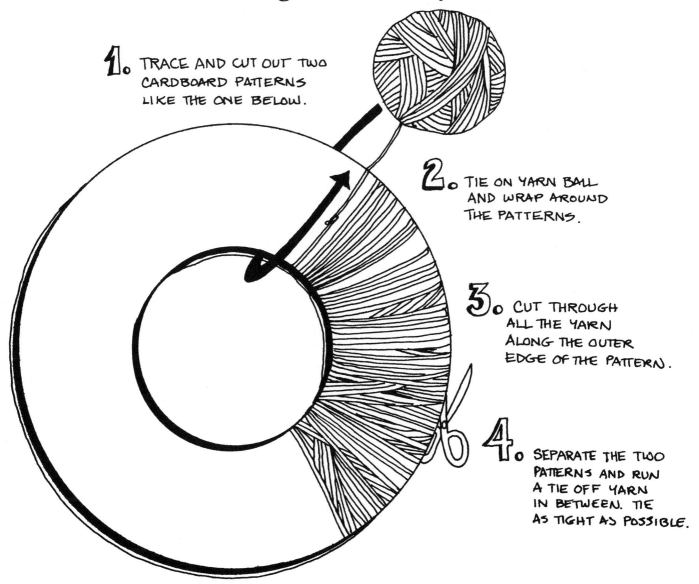

1. TRACE AND CUT OUT TWO CARDBOARD PATTERNS LIKE THE ONE BELOW.

2. TIE ON YARN BALL AND WRAP AROUND THE PATTERNS.

3. CUT THROUGH ALL THE YARN ALONG THE OUTER EDGE OF THE PATTERN.

4. SEPARATE THE TWO PATTERNS AND RUN A TIE OFF YARN IN BETWEEN. TIE AS TIGHT AS POSSIBLE.

5. PULL OUT PATTERNS, AND GIVE YOUR WARM FUZZY A "HAIRCUT" TO EVEN THE FUZZ.

6. DECORATE WITH FELT EYES, MOUTH, PIPE CLEANER ARMS & LEGS.

Warm Fuzzybag

Grades: 1-4
Time: two 20-minute periods
Grouping: full or tribes
Materials: felt bags or envelopes,
           pencils, pens, paper

Objectives

1. To build group inclusion
2. To reinforce the concept of appreciation
3. To build self-esteem

Instructions

1. Have each person make a "warm fuzzy" bag with his/her name printed on it.
2. Ask each person to write at least one warm fuzzy to each member of the total group. (Since this exercise is time consuming, it is suggested that the remaining instructions be completed another day.)
3. Hide each person's warm fuzzy bag prior to continuing the exercise.
4. Have each person locate his/her bag.
5. After all bags have been located, place them on table and instruct people to place their warm fuzzy messages in the appropriate bags.

Discussion

Ask questions such as:
- Would you want people to know which warm fuzzy you gave them?
- What warm fuzzy would you like to give yourself?

Reflection

Ask questions such as:
- How do you feel about receiving such nice messages?
- Would you like it if people gave warm fuzzies more often?

Appreciation

Invite statements of appreciation:
- "I liked it when . . ."

Objectives

1. To build inclusion and sense of community
2. Practice active listening

Instructions

1. Ask participants to sit in one large circle.
2. Explain that during this activity each person will have an opportunity to share his name and something special about himself. Give people a minute to think of something special.
3. Begin the activity by stating your name and something about yourself: "My name is Sue, and I am wonderful at organizing things." Then, while holding onto the end of the yarn roll the yarn ball to someone across from you in the circle. This process continues until all have either shared or passed, and a "spider web" pattern has been created.

Discussion

Ask questions such as:
- How might we symbolically interpret this "spider web"? note symbolism, design, community involvement etc.
- What helps to build community when people get together?

After brief discussion, to unravel spider web, have last person toss ball to connecting person, and when doing so repeat that person's name and perhaps special quality. Continue the process until spider web is unwound and ball back to you.

Reflection

Ask questions such as:
- Does anyone miss the spider web? How do you feel now?
- Do you feel different than when we started the activity?
- Was it difficult to remember names and personal data?
- Would anyone like to share an "I learned" statement?

Appreciation

Suggest people make statements of appreciation:
- "I liked it when you said . . ."
- "I'm a lot like you when . . ."
- "I admire you for . . ."

Spider Web

Grades: K-adult
Time: Depending on group size
Grouping: full community
Materials: ball of colored yarn

Name Game

Grades: K-adult
Time: depending on group size
Grouping: full, tribe
Materials: none

Objectives

1. To "break the ice" for new group people
2. To help people learn first-names
3. To build inclusion and self-esteem

Instructions

1. Have everyone sit in one large circle.
2. Ask first person to say: Example: "I'm Todd."
3. Ask second person to say first person's name and then his own: "You're Todd, I'm Scott."
4. Third person repeats sequence: "You're Todd, you're Scott, and I'm Karen."
5. Process continues around circle until everyone has participated. The last person says everyone's name.

Variation: Use alliterative adjectives ("Terrific Todd"); favorite foods ("Ice Cream Todd"), activities ("Football Todd"), etc.

Discussion

Ask questions such as:
- Why does a person like being called by his first name?
- How many of us will now be able to remember many people's first names during our time together today?

Reflection

Ask questions:
- How did you feel as your turn came closer?
- How did the group react if a member was temporarily stumped on a name?
- How do we feel as a group now?

Appreciation

Suggest people make statements of appreciation:
- "I felt good when . . ."
- "I like the way . . ."

Three Tribles*

Grades: K-adult
Time: 15 minutes
Grouping: full or tribes
Materials: three tribles

Objectives

1. To build inclusion and affection in full group
2. To share current feelings
3. To give and accept appreciation

Instructions

1. Have people sit in full circle.
2. Talk about how we all arrived today with different feelings: some of us are happy and excited; some of us are feeling sad, tired, angry; and some of us just feel kind of in between in our emotions: not happy, not sad, just here.
3. Pass out the three Tribles (which you have prepared earlier, one for each person).
4. Ask people to look at the three Tribles and decide which face looks most like they feel right now.
5. Review Tribe norms.
6. As the teacher or facilitator share first to model activity. Be honest. Share which face you feel like and why.
7. Go around the circle, each person having an opportunity to share or pass. If many pass, go around again until you feel that all who wish to share have done so.

Discussion

Ask questions related to content of what was shared: "Is there someone who will help you fix your bike, Susan?" Encourage others to do the same.

Reflection

Ask questions such as:
- Do you feel differently now than you did when we began sharing?
- How was it, sharing your Trible with the class?
- What were some of the feelings people shared?

Appreciation

Ask people to comment:
- "I felt like you when . . ."
- "I liked it when . . ."

*A Trible is a warm fuzzy, loving creature which first appeared from outer space in the television program **Star Trek**.

Pattern to Make THREE TRIBLES

Objectives

1. To practice components of attentive listening:
   - Use of silence
   - Non-verbal encouragement
   - Paraphrasing
   - Reflecting feelings
2. To share ideas and feelings about any given topic.
3. To build inclusion

I Hear You!

Grades: 6-adult
Time: 30 minutes per person
Grouping: tribe
Materials: none

Instructions

1. Discuss and demonstrate listening skills (refer to Chapter 3).
2. Ask students to form triads and designate each member as an A, B or C. Ask for a show of hands of all A's, B's and all C's to avoid confusion.
3. Explain that each person will have an opportunity to play each role in his/her triad; round 1, A will observe, B will be the speaker and C the listener. Post this chart.

	A	B	C
Round 1	Observer	Speaker	Listener
Round 2	Speaker	Listener	Observer
Round 3	Listener	Observer	Speaker

5. Give speakers a topic of your choice to speak on for 5 minutes (Example: "Should students be allowed to vote?").
6. Ask listener to practice one or two (no more than two) components of active listening.
7. Ask observers to pay attention to the interaction, and after 5 minutes, give feedback to the listener. (Include what they saw the listener doing both verbally and non-verbally, and their observations of how the speaker responded.)
8. Repeat the process until all participants have had an opportunity to practice all skills.

Discussion

Ask questions such as:
- What types of things did people share?
- Was it easy or difficult to talk about . . . ?

Reflection

Ask questions such as:
- What was it like to be listened to in that way?
- What was it like to use these skills?
- What did observers see that was positive or negative?

Appreciation

Suggest people make statements of appreciation:
- "I felt good when . . ."
- "I liked it when . . ."

Meet Someone Special

Grades: K-adult
Time: 20-30 minutes
Grouping: dyads and full group
Materials: none

Objectives

1. To introduce people to a large group
2. To build community inclusion
3. To build self-esteem and appreciation for a person's uniqueness

Instructions

1. This is a good activity to help brand new groups of people be introduced to each other. Have everyone seated in a full circle while you give directions.
2. Review the tribe norms.
3. Ask people to stand up and look about for someone they do not know well. Tell them to invite such a person to be his/her partner.
4. Have each person interview the other one for ten minutes, listening attentively so they will remember important unique qualities and details about the person; at the end of 10 minutes have the partners switch roles.
5. After the stated time is again up, call the dyads back to the full group and ask each person to introduce the person he/she interviewed by sharing the special things learned.

Discussion

- Is it unusual for people to take the time to do this in new groups? In organizations? In community meetings? Why don't they?
- How do you think it would help people?

Reflection

- How did you feel being interviewed by your partner?
- What was it like to be an interviewer?
- How do you feel now in contrast to when you first arrived?
- Did you choose your partner or were you chosen?
- What have you learned about yourself?

Appreciation

- "I appreciated it when . . ."
- "I liked it when . . ."

People Puzzles

Grades: K-adult
Time: 20 minutes
Grouping: tribes
Materials: picture, puzzles

Objectives

1. To build inclusion
2. To form or announce membership in tribes

Instructions

1. Pre-prepare one puzzle for each group or tribe. Cut puzzle into the number of pieces to match the number of people that will be in each respective tribe.
2. Put all the pieces of all the puzzles in a box and have each person take one.
3. Ask participants to circulate and find the puzzle pieces which match the ones they are carrying. They are not to talk while doing this. When their group's puzzle has been completed, then they may talk.
4. Once all of the puzzles have been completed, you may choose to have each group make up a story relating to the picture they have formed. Have each group select one member to be a storyteller and tell the group's story to the whole class.

Discussion

Ask questions such as:
- What made the task difficult? Easy?
- Was this a good way to find people who would be in your group?

Reflection

- What feelings did you have when you began the task? How do you feel now?
- How did you react to people whose pieces did not fit yours? To those whose pieces did fit?
- What was the atmosphere like in the room?
- What did you talk about when the puzzle was complete?

Appreciation

- "I liked it when . . ."
- "I'm a lot like you when . . ."
- "I admire you for . . ."

Wishful Thinking

Grades: K-adult
Time: depending on group size
Grouping: tribe
Materials: none

Objectives

1. To provide opportunity to express a wish
2. To experience group acceptance of a concern

Instructions

1. Have members sit or stand in a circle.
2. Ask each person to make a brief statement beginning with "I wish . . ." Instruct all that there is no discussion during activity. Statements can be related to part of personal life, feelings about politics, school, the group, etc.
3. If possible have groups share around circle more than once.

Discussion

Ask such questions as:
- When was the last time you were encouraged to express a wish or share a concern?
- Do we share some common wishes?

Reflection

- How did you feel?
- Did the others listen? How did you know?
- Did people seem more willing to share as the activity progressed?

Appreciation

Invite statements of appreciation:
- "I liked it when . . ."
- "I felt good when . . ."
- "I admired your honesty when . . ."

Objectives

1. To build group inclusion
2. To encourage sharing of positive feelings

Instructions

1. Have people sit or stand in a large circle.
2. Ask each to share one positive experience that happened during the past week. Instruct all that there will be no discussion until all have shared.

Discussion

Ask questions such as:
- Were there any similarities about the "good things" shared?
- When was the last time you told someone about a positive experience?

Reflection

- Was it hard to think of something good to share?
- Did other people listen carefully? How did you know?
- Did people share more freely as the activity progressed?

Appreciation

- "I liked it when . . ."
- "I'm like you when . . ."
- "I felt good when . . ."

Something Good

Grades: K-adult
Time: depending on group size
Grouping: full community
Materials: none

Singing The Blues

Grades: K-3
Time: 20-30 minutes
Grouping: full group
Materials: none or a guitar

Objectives

1. To promote commonality and group cohesion
2. To introduce sharing of troubles in a non-threatening, enjoyable way
3. To channel group energy

Instructions

1. Ask group if they know what "the blues" are. State that in this activity, the "blues" are feeling badly about something.
2. Ask if anyone has the blues and why.
3. Sing or strum a melody which is simple and fun. (Example: A seven year-old boy says his dog was hurt. Words could be: "I've got the blues, I've got the blues, I've got the my dog was hurt blues").
4. Ask everyone to join in singing.
5. Share one of your own blues first. Lead singing on it.
6. Invite others to tell their blues and lead singing.
7. Discourage people from making fun of another's troubles. Help them to understand it's a put-down to do so.

Discussion

Ask questions such as:

- Were you surprised that everyone seems to sometimes have the "blues"?
- Is it easier to talk/sing about blues than about feeling good?

Reflection

Ask questions:

- How was it to sing together? Too loud? Just right?
- Do you feel different after "singing your blues"?
- Would you like to sing about "good times"?

Appreciation

Invite statements of appreciation:

- "I enjoyed singing because . . ."
- "I feel like you do when . . ."

Objectives

1. To promote appreciation of personal qualities
2. To encourage respect for others
3. To build inclusion

Instructions

1. Have people meet in tribes
2. Distribute materials
3. Have people write their first names in big colorful letters going down the left margin side of the paper.
4. Draw or cut out adjectives (descriptive words or phrases) that begin with the letters of your first name and that describe your special qualities.
   P   playful, powerful
   A   active
   T   talkative, tidy
   T   terrific
   I   interesting
5. Ask people to share their "Names in Print" to the rest of the group.
6. Remind listeners to give full attention to the speaker.
   Questions or comments may be posed at the end of each presentation.

Discussion

- Was it easy or hard to find adjectives for your name?
- How did this activity help you to understand others?

Reflection

- How did you feel when you shared?
- What adjectives did you like best?
- Why?
- Did the group listen?

Appreciation

Invite statements of appreciation:

- "_____, I liked it when you said . . ."
- "_____, I learned that you are . . ."
- "_____, I'm glad that we both have _____ in common."

My Name In Print

Grades: 3-5
Time: 30-60 minutes
Grouping: tribe
Materials: 9 × 12 construction paper, magazines, scissors, glue, colored marking pens

Interview Circle

Grades: K-adult
Time: 15-30 minutes
Grouping: full or tribes
Materials: none

Objectives

1. To build inclusion and influence
2. To enhance communication skills
3. To share personal beliefs, feelings and interests

Instructions

1. Ask all to sit or stand in large community circle.
2. Explain that we will interview a person who will sit in the center of the circle by asking him only three questions. The person will choose the questions from people who raise their hands. He has the right to "pass" on any questions that he chooses not to answer.
3. Model the activity first by being in the center and responding to three questions yourself.
4. Questions may be autobiographical or may relate to issues, curriculum, politics, hobbies, friendship, sports, etc.

Discussion

- Did this activity help you to know group members better?
- Can we generalize about the types of questions asked?

Reflection

- How did you feel being interviewed?
- Did the group listen? How did you know?

Appreciation

Invite statements of appreciation:
- "I liked it when . . ."
- "I admired your honesty when . . ."

Objectives

1. To energize a group
2. To promote inclusion
3. To experience the fun and creative power of brainstorming as a problem-solving technique

Instructions

1. Ask each tribe to appoint a recorder to jot down ideas on paper, blackboard, or newsprint as fast as ideas are called out. (With very young children use an aide or older student.)
2. Instruct tribes on rules that they need to follow in order to "brainstorm."
   D. defer judgement
   O. off-beat, original
   V. vast number
   E. expand, elaborate
3. Tell groups that they have five minutes to call out and write down as many ideas as possible on the subject: "How could we design a better bathtub . . . one for more enjoyment, efficiency, and comfort than ordinary tubs?" Recorder jots down all ideas.
4. Stop the brainstorming at five minutes. Ask each recorder to read list. Lead applause after each group's creativity.

Discussion

Ask questions such as:
- Are many heads better than one to get a wider range of ideas?
- What would have happened if we had judged, commented or discussed ideas as they were offered?
- Could we use this technique on other questions? Can you suggest some?

Reflection

Ask questions:
- Did you feel free to offer any silly suggestions without judging them yourself?
- Was it difficult not to judge or comment?
- Did the group have fun?
- How does the group feel about itself after this activity?

Appreciation

Invite statements of appreciation:
- "I liked it when you said . . ."
- "I felt good when . . ."
- "Your suggestions helped me to . . ."

Build A Better Bathtub

Grades: K-adult
Time: 20 minutes
Grouping: tribe
Materials: felt markers, large sheets of paper

Chain Reaction

Grades: K-adult
Time: 15-30 minutes
Grouping: tribes
Materials: no

Objectives

1. To build inclusion and influence
2. To increase communication skills
3. To provide opportunity to share personal interests, opinions and ideas.
4. To involve cooperative learning groups in asking each other questions about subject matter.

Instructions

1. Have people meet in tribes.
2. Remind all of their "right to pass," and to honor the other norms.
3. Have one group member ask a question of another. The interviewee answers questions and then asks another question of a third person. Chain continues in this manner.
4. Questions may be of an autobiographical nature, deal with a number of issues (politics, hobbies, education, friendship, family interests), or curriculum. This is a good activity to help prepare for a test.
5. Remind group members to give full, caring attention.

Discussion

- Did this activity help you to know group members better?
- Was it difficult to think of questions to ask each other?

Reflection

- How did you feel when it was your turn?
- Did the group listen? How did you know?

Appreciation

Invite statements of appreciation:
- "I liked it when . . ."
- "I admired your honesty when . . ."

Objectives

1. To promote an awareness of one's own level self-esteem
2. To compare image of oneself with other's expectations
3. To foster positive feelings about group members

Instructions

1. Have people sit in tribes and pass out Self-Esteem Assessment Charts.
2. Briefly discuss what self-esteem is and importance of it.
3. Allow 5–10 minutes to complete the charts
4. Remind people of the norms and ask people to share their charts with the members of their tribe. Suggest that they explain details and comparisons between "Your opinion of self" and "Others expectations."
5. Lead a full group discussion after tribal sharing.

Discussion

- Have you ever had the opportunity before to think about how you see yourself in comparison with others?
- What similarities did you notice with other group members?
- What did you learn about yourself?

Reflection

- What feelings came up for you as you shared your chart?
- Was it difficult to complete the chart? Why?
- How do you feel now?

Appreciation

- "I liked it when you . . ."
- "I respect how you . . ."
- "I think you're neat because . . ."

Self-Esteem Assessment

Grades: 5-adult
Time: 30 minutes
Grouping: full or tribes
Materials: Self-esteem assessment chart

Self-Esteem Assessment Chart

	Your Opinion of Yourself	**Expectations You Believe Others Have**
Your Intelligence		
Your Appearance		
Your Ability to Relate to Others		
Your Future Ambitions		
Your Personality		
Your Role as a Male Your Role as a Female		
Your Role as a Daughter Your Role as a Son		
Your Physical Health		
Your Having or Developing Talents		
Your Ability to Complete Tasks		

Sharing From A Sack

Grades: K-6
Time: 20-50 minutes
Grouping: full group or tribes
Materials: each person brings an
              object in a paper sack

Objectives

1. To give each person an opportunity to share something special or meaningful of himself
2. To build inclusion
3. To practice active listening
4. To practice oral presentation of self

Instructions

1. Several days before this activity is to be done, ask each child to choose a special object to bring from home. The object may represent a hobby, interests, award or symbol of a personal quality. Tell people to bring the object concealed in a paper sack.
2. Have participants form one large circle.
3. Going around the circle, ask each person to share his/her object by removing it from the sack and saying how the object is representative of him.

Discussion

Ask questions such as:
   • Did you like sharing your objects?
   • How did you decide which object to bring?

Reflection

   • What feelings did you have as you listened to others?
   • How do you feel about the object you brought? Do you wish you had chosen something different?

Appreciation

Invite statements of appreciation:
   • "_____, you seem to love your hobby. Can I do it with you sometime?"
   • "_____, I liked it when you said . . ."
   • "_____, thank you for listening . . ."

Shoe 'n Tell: Variations On Sharing From A Sack

Grades: K-6
Time: 50 minutes
Grouping: full
Materials: each person brings a pair
of shoes enclosed in a
paper sack

Instructions

1. Ask each person to choose a pair of his/her shoes and bring them from home and enclosed in a paper sack. (Allow a few days.)
2. Have full group sit in a circle.
3. Sharing from the sack could take on any of these forms:
   • How these shoes serve me to do things that I like to do.
   • Sharing from the point of view of the shoe . . . what it's like being the shoe that belongs to the person sharing.
   • Sharing from the point of view of the shoe . . . how I'd like to be taken care of if I could have it my way.

After exercise is completed follow with discussion, reflection and appreciation as suggested in "Sharing from a Sack."

SINCE WE'RE NEIGHBORS LET'S BE FRIENDS ♪♪

"Am I Napoleon?"

Grades: K-adult
Time: 20 minutes
Grouping: full
Materials: 3″ × 5″ index cards, common pins, crayon or felt pen

Objective

1. To build inclusion
2. To identify and learn about famous people in history, politics, science or other curricula

Instructions

1. Give each person a 3″ × 5″ index card, a common pin and a pencil.
2. Ask each participant to print, on the card in large block letters, the name of some famous person, living or dead. Used with small children, animals, plants, fruits may be used.
3. Ask each person to pin his or her "famous person" card on the back of another person, but not to let that person know what name has been pinned to their clothing.
4. Tell people to find out who they are by milling around and asking other people "Am I _____?" Only one question at a time may be asked of another as people seek either a "yes" and "no" answer. The process continues until all have identified their famous names.

Discussion

Ask questions:
- What were some of the "famous names" used?
- What kinds of questions did people ask?
- What do you know about the person who was on your back. Share all you know with someone else.

Reflection

- Do you identify with your "famous name" in any way?
- Why was it difficult (or easy) to find out "who you were"?
- What are your feelings toward the group now?

Appreciation

Invite statements of appreciation:
- "I liked it when . . ."
- "I'm a lot like you when . . ."

Tribal Portrait

Grades: K-adults
Time: varies (see note*)
Grouping: tribes
Materials: butcher paper, felt pens, pencils, erasers

Objectives

1. To develop self-awareness
2. To develop awareness of spatial relationships
3. To develop cooperative skills
4. To practice observation skills

Instructions

1. Explain to the full group that each tribe will draw a group portrait. The portrait will include individual pictures of each member.
2. Ask people to meet in tribes, get material and find a space to work.
3. Each tribe member asks one other member to do a sketch of him/her.
4. Artists draw their subjects using pencils.
5. After completing portrait, artists check with subjects for additions or corrections.
6. After corrections and additions have been made, the artists use marking pens on portrait.
7. When every tribe member has a portrait finished, the tribe decides how they will present their "tribal portrait" to the rest of the class.

Discussion

Ask questions such as:
- Which people look like themselves?
- Which tribe took the longest time to finish?

Reflection

Ask questions:
- What feelings did you have while your portrait was being drawn?
- What feelings did you have when you saw your portrait?

Appreciation

Invite statements of appreciation:
- "When I look at our tribal portrait I feel . . ."
- "I like what you drew because . . ."

---

*Note:

This project can best be done over a period of 2-5 days because of attention span. Also the teacher needs to move from tribe to tribe giving some instruction in the drawing techniques needed. Excellent opportunity to bring in outside Art resource person to work with small groups.

Tee-Shirts

Grades: 3-adult
Time: 40 minutes
Grouping: tribes
Materials: tee-shirt worksheet, colored pens or crayons, pencils

Objectives

1. To build inclusion
2. To practice communication and listening skills

Instructions

1. Distribute copies of T-Shirt worksheets (see next page), pencils, and colored pens.
2. Ask each participant to print his/her name across the center of the tee-shirt, then . . .
   - On the left sleeve write or draw: two things you do well
   - On the right sleeve: something you like about being your age right now
   - On the collar: a word you'd like people to say when they describe you
   - On the left lower side: a wish you have for yourself
   - On the right lower side: something you want to be or do when you grow up
   - In center under name: something you like to do in free time
3. Ask participants to form small groups.
4. Have each in turn share his/her tee-shirt with the other group members.
5. Ask listeners to give full, undivided, caring attention to the speaker.

There are endless other fine questions for this activity: someone you admire, a quality you like in a friend, something you want to learn, favorite subject or book, etc. Select those most appropriate for group's age and culture.

Discussion

Ask questions such as:
- What did you learn about your tribe members that you did not know before?
- Any similarities among group members' hopes?

Reflection

Ask questions such as:
- How did you feel sharing about yourself?
- Were people listening? How could you tell?

Appreciation

- "I like it when . . ."
- "I'm glad you're . . ."

Tee-Shirt Worksheet

Objectives

1. Language development
2. Cooperative skills
3. Large motor development

Make a Machine

Grades: 2-adult
Time: 20 minutes
Grouping: full
Materials: none

Instructions

1. Have the class sit in a large circle.
2. Ask one person to begin making some movement (no sound).
3. Tell the next person to make a movement that connects with the first person (touching knees or hands or heads, etc.)
4. Ask people to continue to join the "machine" one at a time and when all are part of it to keep moving as one great machine.
5. If some people choose to pass, affirm it is O.K.; have them move out of the circle but observe.
6. Stop the movement. Go around again, this time each person adds sound to their movement.
7. Move the "machine" around the classroom, perhaps even out into the hallway, around the school!

Discussion

Ask questions such as:
- What did you see?
- What could we call our machine?
- What would it's purpose be?

Reflection

- What did you feel doing it?
- Was anyone shy or embarrassed?

Appreciation

- "I liked our big machine because . . ."
- "This was fun because . . ."

Note: Follow up inventions for curricula are naturals (science art, engineering)

Bumper Sticker

Grades: 2-adult
Time: 30 minutes
Grouping: full or tribe
Materials: strips of colored paper, colored crayons or markers

Objectives

1. To present something special about oneself
2. To build inclusion
3. To encourage attentive listening

Instructions

1. Give each person a long strip of paper and a felt marker or crayon with which to create a "bumper sticker" which he or she would enjoy displaying on his/her automobile bumper (wagon, bicycle etc.)
2. Have each person in turn share his or her bumper sticker with the rest of the group. Remind people they have the right to pass.
3. Remind all to give full attention to the speaker. After all have shared, people may ask questions, express mutual feelings and concerns.

Discussion

Ask questions such as:
- Can we generalize about the kinds of things people put on their bumper stickers?
- Would anyone like to share something special he learned about another person?
- How did this activity help you know people better?

Reflection

Ask questions such as:
- Would you display your bumper sticker on your family's auto bumper?
- How did you feel as you shared?
- Did the group listen to you as you shared? How did you know?
- Did you have fun?

Appreciation

Invite statements of appreciation:
- "I liked it when . . ."
- "I admired you for . . ."

Objectives

1. To increase awareness of importance of stating appreciation
2. To practice the norms
3. To provide for an initial inclusion activity

Instructions

1. Pass out the appreciation worksheet to all class members.
2. Post a large visual of the worksheet in the front of the room from which you may work as a model.
3. Ask people to fill in each of the four boxes of the worksheet with one positive statement to self, best friend, Mom and/or Dad and a classmate. Suggest that they use some of the positive statement forms noted on the bottom of the worksheet.
4. Ask people to meet in tribes to share their positive statements.
5. Have each person circle with a felt pen the core of each of their positive statements, such as: "Mom, I appreciate it when you **listen to my problems**."
6. Have one member of each tribe record all the core ideas (that are included on people's worksheets.
7. Ask the recorder from each tribe to report the summaries to the whole class.

Discussion

Ask questions such as:
- Why is it important to make statements of appreciation to others?
- When do you say the things your wrote on your worksheet?

Reflection

Ask questions such as:
- Was it hard to think of positive statements?
- Which of the four statements that you wrote would you feel good about if it was said to you?

Appreciation

Invite statements of appreciation:
- "I liked it when . . ."
- "Thank you for . . ."

Appreciating Others

Grades: 2-adult
Time: 45 minutes
Grouping: tribes
Materials: Appreciating Others worksheets, pencils, large paper, felt pens

Tribes Program Handout

Appreciating Others

Self	**Best Friend**
Mom/Dad	**Classmate**

Suggested positive statement forms:

_____, I liked it when you . . .

_____, I appreciate it when . . .

_____, I'm glad you . . .

_____, I want to give you a warm fuzzy because . . .

_____, thanks for . . .

Objectives

1. To make statements of appreciation
2. To build self-esteem
3. To build inclusion

Instructions

1. Prepare posterboard cut-outs similar to the one on the next page for each participant.
2. Ask participants to meet in tribes.
3. Have each person write his/her name in large colorful letters on the head area of the cut-outs.
4. Instruct people to pass the cut-outs around the circle so that each member can write a positive statement on the cut-outs. When all have done so, ask each person to write a "boaster" about himself on his own card.

Discussion

Ask questions such as:
- Did you notice any similarities among the cards that you saw?
- Did you learn anything new about people in your group?

Reflection

- How did you feel when you knew that someone else was writing on your card?
- How did you feel when you read the comments on your card?

Appreciation

Invite statements of appreciation:
- "I'm glad you notice that I . . ."
- "I felt good when . . ."

Boasters

Grades: 2-adult
Time: 45 minutes
Grouping: sub-groups, tribes
Materials: 12 inch high posterboard cutouts of side views of a child or older person

Tribe Program Handout

Boasters

Something I Cherish

Grades: 2-adult
Time: 20 minutes
Grouping: full, sub-group, tribe
Materials: none

Objectives

1. To increase communication skills
2. To build inclusion

Instructions

1. Ask people to form triads.
2. Ask each person to take a turn sharing with other two: "One thing that I cherish is . . . ," explaining why it is so special, why she wants others to know, etc.
3. To draw the triads back into larger group setting, have each small group member share with full group one item a member of his triad cherishes. Every participant speaks of another and is spoken about by a member of his triad.

Discussion

Ask questions such as:
- Can we make some generalizations about the type of things people seem to cherish most?
- Can you think of other things we could share, such as "A place I cherish . . . ," "A person I cherish . . . ?"

Appreciation

Invite statements of appreciation:
- "I liked it when . . ."
- "I felt good when . . ."
- "I was interested when . . ."

"I'm Proud"... Appreciation Circle

Grades: 2-adult
Time: 30 minutes
Grouping: full, tribe
Materials: none

Objectives

1. To encourage sharing of good feelings about one's self
2. To encourage acceptance and appreciation of others

Instructions

1. Each tribe sits in a circle with one tribe member in the middle as "the focus person."
2. The focus person makes an "I'm proud" statement such as:
   "I'm proud that I am . . ."
   "I'm proud that I am able to . . ."
   "I'm proud that I . . ."
3. Tribe members then make statements of positive feedback or appreciation to the focus person.
4. Each takes his/her turn at being the focus.

Discussion

Ask questions such as:
- How did you choose your "I'm proud" statement?
- Did you learn anything new about each other?

Reflection

Ask questions such as:
- How did you feel when you gave and received statements of appreciation?
- How do you all feel about each other now?

Appreciation

Invite people to make statements of appreciation:
- Is there anyone who would like to make a statement to anyone else in the class?

All In The Family

Grades: 2-adult
Time: 20 minutes
Grouping: sub-group
Materials: none

Objectives

1. To build group inclusion
2. To promote awareness of how other family members feel

Instructions

1. Ask people to form groups in different parts of the room according to their birth position in their family: eldest, youngest, in-betweens, only child.
2. Share with other members of your group:
   • How does it feel to be (first born?) . . .
   • What responsibilities did you have?
   • What advantages did you have?
3. Merge two groups together so eldest are with in-betweens and only children with youngest. (Mix groups together whichever way you want.)
4. Now ask these groups to share:
   • Who did you think had more power in the family?
   • How did you feel toward other siblings?
   • Who got attention in your family and how did they get it?

Discussion

Ask questions such as:
   • What did you learn?
   • Were there any surprises?
   • Can we make generalizations about birth positions?

Reflection

Ask questions such as:
   • Did you identify with anyone else in the group?
   • How did you feel being with others in the same birth position as you?
   • Did you feel a common bond with those in the same birth position as you?

Appreciation

Invite statements of appreciation:
   • "I'm a lot like you when . . ."
   • "I felt good when . . ."

They Call Me . . .

Grades: 3-adult
Time: 20 minutes
Grouping: tribes
Materials: "What's In My Name?" worksheet

Objectives

1. To initiate tribe inclusion
2. To encourage group members to share feelings
3. To practice attentive listening

Instructions

1. Ask each person complete the following "homework" assignment:

   Find out from your parents how you were named. Were you named after someone? How was your name picked? (You may want to send home a dittoed instruction sheet for younger children.) Allow a few days for your class to complete the assignment.

2. Have people meet in tribes.

3. Ask each person to take a turn sharing how his/her name was selected, what nicknames may have happened, and how he/she feels about the name or nicknames.

Discussion

Ask questions such as:

- Did you notice any similarities in how names were selected for people?
- Did this activity help you to know each other better? How?

Reflection

Ask questions such as:

- Did people seem pleased with their names?
- As you listened, were you moved by anyone's feelings about his/her name?
- Would you ever consider changing your name? Why?

Appreciation

Invite statements of appreciation:

- "_____, I liked what you said about your name because . . ."
- "_____, I like your name because . . ."
- "_____, I felt that you understood when I said . . ."

Tribes Program Handout

NAME _____

What's in My Name?

Instructions:

Answer the following questions about your name. Interview your parents if you do not know all the answers.

1. Why did your parents choose your name?

2. If you were named after someone, who was it?

3. What nick-names do you have, and how did you get them?

4. Do you like your name? Why, or why not?

5. If you could choose another name, what would it be?

Self-Esteem Cards

Grades: 3-adult
Time: 15 minutes
Grouping: tribe
Materials: 3 × 5 index cards

Objectives

1. To build self-esteem
2. To reinforce the concept of appreciation
3. To foster positive feelings among tribe members

Instructions

1. Activity should take place after tribe members know one another fairly well.
2. Instruct each member to write his/her first name in upper corner of card.
3. Tell tribes to place all cards in a center pile, and have each member draw a card (not divulging whose card he has), and then writing a thoughtful, warm statement about person whose name is on the card.
4. Return all cards to the central pile and repeat the process of drawing and writing 4 or 5 additional times.
5. After the final writing, return all cards and draw again. This time instruct each member to read all the remarks written on the card to the whole tribe . . . delivering the group's message as warmly and sincerely as possible.

Discussion

Ask questions such as:
- When was the last time you received written warm statements like these?
- Do people usually remember to say nice things about others?

Reflection

Ask questions such as:
- How do you feel?
- How do you feel about the tribe?

Appreciation

Invite statements of appreciation:
- "I felt good when . . ."
- "Thank you for . . ."

On My Back

Grades: 3-adult
Time: 20 minutes
Grouping: tribe or full group
Materials: Butcher paper, tape, felt markers

Objectives

1. To build self-esteem
2. To encourage giving statements of appreciation
3. To structure learning about well-known characters in history, politics, current events, literature etc.

Instructions

1. Give each tribe member a large piece of butcher paper, a felt marker, and two pieces of masking tape.
2. Ask each person to print the following phrase at the top of the paper: "I like (name of person or famous character) because . . ."
3. Ask each child to use the masking tape to have another person attach the paper to his/her shoulders so that it hangs down like a cape on her back.
4. Have people stand and circulate about so that each person in the group can write a statement of appreciation on other people's backs.
5. After all have written, ask people to sit down in tribe circle, have each person remove his/her paper, and give it to someone else in the tribe to read aloud. (Feel free to devise other ways to share the statements, depending on trust level of the group.)
6. If the activity has been about each person (rather than famous character) encourage people to save their posters, perhaps to put on the walls of their bedrooms at home.

Discussion

Ask questions like:
- What are some of the neat things people wrote?
- Do we often take the time to say things like this to one another? Why or why not?

Reflection

Ask questions like:
- What feelings did you have when people were writing on your paper?
- What feelings did you have when your validation statements were being read aloud?
- Did you have any trouble thinking of things to write? Why or why not?

Appreciation

Invite statements of appreciation:
- "I like it when . . ."
- "I felt good when . . ."

People Hunt

Grades: 3-adult
Time: 40 minutes
Grouping: full or sub-group
Materials: People Hunt sheets, I, II, III, pencils

Objectives

1. To promote community inclusion
2. To introduce self to others
3. To encourage sharing information
4. To structure learning about well-known characters in history, politics, current events, literature etc.

Instructions

1. Give one-third of the group sheet I, one third sheet II, and the remainder sheet III, and pencils as needed.
2. Explain that participants are to circulate around the room finding out the answers to the questions on their sheets. As one person approaches another he/she should introduce him/her self by name. Inform people in advance that they will have 15 minutes.
3. After 10 to 15 minutes ask participants to meet in tribes or form groups of five for discussion/reflection/appreciation.

Discussion

Ask questions such as:
- How willing were you to get up and go around to ask questions?
- Did most people come to you or did you go to them?
- Did you learn anything that impressed or surprised you?

Reflection

- What were you feeling when you went up to people?
- Do you feel any different now from when you first walked in the room?

Appreciation

Invite statements of appreciation:
- "I liked it when you . . ."
- "I felt good when . . ."
- "I'm like you when . . ."

People Hunt I
FIND:

1. A person who does not own a T.V.

His/her name is _____

2. A person whose birthday is within a month after yours.

His/her name is _____

3. A person who can cross his/her eyes.

His/her name is _____

4. A person who traveled over 2,000 miles last summer.

His/her name is _____

5. A person who lives in a house where no one smokes.

His/her name is _____

6. A person who owns a horse.

His/her name is _____

7. A person who is new to this school.

His/her name is _____

8. A person who loves to peel oranges.

His/her name is _____

9. A person who is an artist.

His/her name is _____

10. A person who has more than six brothers and sisters.

His/her name is _____

People Hunt II
FIND:

1. A person who can speak two languages.

His/her name is _____

2. A person who has been to a concert.

His/her name is _____

3. A person who has two different colored eyes.

His/her name is _____

4. A person with a new baby in their home.

His/her name is _____

5. A person whose birthday is the same month as yours.

His/her name is _____

6. A person who can roll their tongue.

His/her name is _____

7. A person who has been ice skating this past year.

His/her name is _____

8. A person not born in this country.

His/her name is _____

9. A person who has more than four animals in their home.

His/her name is _____

10. A person who woke up with a smile this morning.

His/her name is _____

People Hunt III
FIND:

1. A person not born in California (New york, Texas, etc.)

His/her name is _____

2. A person who stayed home last summer.

His/her name is _____

3. A person whose birthday is one month before yours.

His/her name is _____

4. A person who is the oldest in their family.

His/her name is _____

5. A person who can touch their nose with their tongue.

His/her name is _____

6. A person who likes to invent things.

His/her name is _____

7. A person whose jogs for exercise.

His/her name is _____

8. A person who has four dogs in their home.

His/her name is _____

9. A person who has been horse back riding in the past three months.

His/her name is _____

10. A person who has planted a tree.

His/her name is _____

Totem Pole

Grades: 3-adult
Time: 45 minutes
Grouping: sub-group, tribe
Materials: Totem Pole Sheet,
       crayons or markers

Objectives

1. To build self-esteem
2. To build inclusion and influence
3. To encourage sharing

Instructions

1. Give each person a Totem Pole worksheet.
2. In each appropriate area of the totem pole, ask people to draw or write answers to following questions:
   a. Three things you're really good at
   b. Your greatest achievement to date
   c. Three things you would like to improve in your life.
   d. What are some words you would like people to use when they describe you?
3. Provide several options for follow-up activities:
   a. Verbal sharing time in tribes or sub-groups
   b. Have full group try to match unsigned Totem Poles with proper "owners"
   c. Write I-Learned statements

Discussion

Ask questions such as:
- Which questions were the most difficult to answer?
- What did you learn about yourself?
- Did your Totem Pole look like this five years ago? Will it look like this in five years?

Reflection

Ask questions such as:
- How did you feel during this activity?
- What thoughts crossed your mind as you worked on your Totem Pole?
- What area(s) of your Totem pole did you choose to share with neighbors while you were drawing it? Why?

Appreciation

Invite appreciation:
- "I felt good when . . ."
- "I was interested when . . ."

Tribes Program

Totem Pole

1

2

3

4

Extended Nametags

Grades: 3-adult
Time: 15 to 25 minutes
Grouping: full group
Materials: 5″ × 8″ cards, pencils, clock

Objectives

1. To promote inclusion
2. To share personal history, interests, beliefs
3. To enhance communication skills

Instructions

1. Distribute 5″ × 8″ cards and pencils.
2. Ask each participant to print first name or nickname in center of card, then . . .
   a. In upper left corner of card, write:
      • place where you spent your happiest summer
      • your favorite place on earth
   b. Lower left corner:
      • the name of a person who has taught you something important
      • the name of your best friend
   c. Lower right corner:
      • the year when you last remember spending three great days in a row
      • the year when you went on a big trip
   d. Upper right corner: three things you are good at
   e. Under your name: the quality you most value in people
3. Ask each participant to form a triad with two others.
4. Explain that each person in triad will have one minute to talk about one corner of the card, and that each will talk about the same corner.
5. Ask triads to decide on a corner.
6. Ask triads to decide who will go first, second, and third.
7. Give signal to begin. Tell them you will announce when one, two and three minutes have elapsed.
8. Give triads two minutes to make statements of appreciation.
      "I liked it when . . ."
      "You're a lot like me when . . ."
      "I admired you for . . ."
9. Form new triads and repeat steps 3 - 8.
10. After two or three triad changes, ask participants to form large circle. Give opportunity for people to share something they learned about someone.

Discussion

Ask questions such as:
   • What happens when people share information? About themselves?
   • What other information might be appropriate for this activity?
   • Was the time limit a help or a hindrance?

Reflection

Ask questions:

- How were decisions made in triads?
- Did the sharing become easier?
- Did people have fun?
- How are people feeling now?

Appreciation

Suggest people make statements of appreciation:

- "I liked hearing . . ."
- "I admire your . . ."

Open Forum

Grades: Grades 3-adult
Time: 30 minutes
Grouping: sub-group, tribe
Materials: none

Objectives

1. To encourage sharing of feelings
2. To encourage acceptance of diverse feelings, beliefs, cultures

Instructions

1. Pose a question of a personal interest nature or on curriculum to the tribe or sub-group and give people time to consider their answers. Possible interest questions:

   What is the best book that you have ever read?
   How do you select your friends?
   What guides your life?
   If you could be an animal for a day what would you be?
   What is the greatest harm one can do towards another? Why?
   For what do you think you would lay down your life?

2. Ask the groups to listen attentively to each person's response. Remind people that they may pass, but if so need to listen attentively. No discussion or follow-up questions are allowed until each participant has had a chance to speak.

3. After going around the circle, encourage people to ask one another follow-up questions and do further sharing.

Discussion

Follow-up questions should relate to the content of the Open Forum topic.

Reflection

Ask questions such as:
- Was anyone uncomfortable with the question? Why?
- Did anyone's response surprise you?
- Can we generalize about the responses?

Appreciation

Invite statements of appreciation:
- "I liked it when . . ."
- "I'm a lot like you when . . ."
- "You're a lot like me when . . ."

Objectives

1. To build self-esteem
2. To build inclusion

Instructions

1. Explain to the full community that everyone will be introducing them-selves to others through "Wanted Posters" which they will create themselves.
2. Give all people a copy of the "Wanted Poster" from the following page, a straight pin and pencil.
3. Allow five to ten minutes for everyone to complete their posters.
4. Have group members help each other pin the posters on their own backs; then tell everyone to circulate around reading each other's posters and sharing their own.
5. Allow sufficient time for all to read each others', and then call the group back to sit in a full circle.
6. Discuss and reflect upon the activity.

Discussion

- What did you learn about other group members?
- What did you learn about yourself?

Reflection

- How did you feel milling around the room?
- What was the most difficult section of the Wanted Poster for you to fill out? Why?
- How do you feel about yourself now?

Appreciation

- "I liked it when . . ."
- "I appreciated that . . ."

Wanted Posters

Grades: 4-adult
Time: 30 minutes
Grouping: full group, dyads, tribes
Materials: Wanted Posters, pins, pencils

Tribes Program Handout

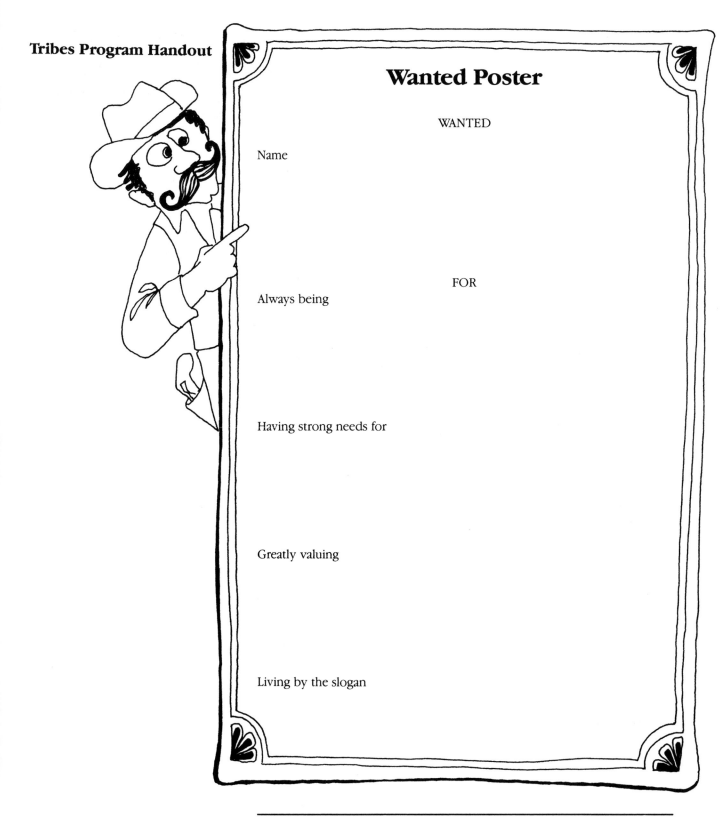

Wanted Poster

WANTED

Name

FOR

Always being

Having strong needs for

Greatly valuing

Living by the slogan

Objectives

1. To explore motives and alternatives concerning the use of cigarettes, alcohol or drugs
2. To develop peer support towards changing norms to non-use
3. To build inclusion in tribes

Instructions

1. Ask each tribe to appoint a recorder and pass out 2 large sheets of butcher paper and felt pens to each tribe.
2. Tell groups that we will be doing a brainstorm; review rules of brainstorming.
3. Ask tribes to brainstorm for five minutes on the subject, "Why people smoke, drink alcohol or use drugs." Ask recorder to jot down all ideas as quickly as they are called out.
4. After five minutes, stop the brainstorming, and have the recorders take new sheets of paper. Ask the tribes now to brainstorm another list, "What are some alternatives to using cigarettes, alcohol or drugs?"
5. Stop the brainstorming after five minutes and have the recorders report back.
6. Ask people to write in their Personal Journals or a contract with themselves stating what they intend to do about using chemical substances and how they would rather live their lives. Have them share their commitments with their tribes.
7. Next ask the tribes to discuss what they are willing to do to help friends in the tribe or elsewhere say "no" to peer pressure on drug use. Have them make a list. Report back.

Discussion

- Do you think drugs are a big health problem in this country
- What are the best ways to do something about it?

Reflection

- Do you feel this was an important activity for you today? Why?
- How do you feel about the commitment that you have written for yourself? Are you willing to help others stay straight too?
- How do you feel about your tribe?

Appreciation

- "It helped me when . . ."
- "I appreciated . . ."

Reasons and Alternatives

Grades: 4-8
Time: 45-60 minutes
Grouping: tribes
Materials: butcher paper markers

Kitchen Kapers

Grades: 3-adult
Time: 20 minutes
Grouping: sub-group, tribe
Materials: 1 packet of materials for each small group

Objectives

1. To build inclusion
2. To experience the creative power of brainstorming as a group problem-solving technique
3. To promote creativity and fun

Instructions

1. Prepare packets containing: 2 index cards, 2 paper clips, 4 toothpicks, and 1 pencil in business-sized envelope. Seal envelope.
2. Have people form sub-groups or meet in tribes.
3. Give each group an envelope of materials. State that they will have 12 minutes to invent and build one "kitchen utensil every household simply must have." Encourage bizarre, zany, and unique ideas.
4. Stop the "inventors" at 12 minutes.
5. Ask each group to then present a short, 3-minute commercial advertising its product.

Discussion

Ask questions such as:
- What other ideas for inventions did your group have?
- Throughout construction, did the purposes for the device change?
- What have we learned about the variety of talent in our groups?
- When was the last time you built something with your hands?
- Did the group have fun?

Reflection

Ask questions:
- Did you feel free to offer suggestions?
- How did your group decide what to build?
- Who was the leader? How did you know?
- How did you feel before the group knew what it would build?
- How did you feel when the device was completed?
- How do you feel as a tribe now?

Appreciation

Invite statements of appreciation:
- "I felt good when . . ."
- "I liked it when . . ."

Objectives

1. To build inclusion
2. To create a visual illustration of one's life
3. To encourage attentive listening

Instructions

1. Ask people to meet in tribes.
2. Give each person a piece of paper and colored crayons with which to draw a visual illustration of her "life to date," the significant trends and patterns of her years thus far in the form of a "map." (Use your own to illustrate.)
3. Invite each person to share his "life map" with other group members, explaining the rationale for "road signs," "place names," ups and downs, and so on.
4. Ask people to give their full, undivided, caring attention to the speaker; after each person's ask group members to draw out more details, ask questions, express their mutual feelings or concerns.

Discussion

Ask questions such as:
- When was the last time you shared something of your life with others?
- Any similarities among group members' experiences? Differences?
- Did this activity help you to know group members better?
- Did we learn anything about the group as a whole?

Reflection

Ask questions such as:
- How did you feel as you made your "life map"? As you shared with the group?
- Did the group listen while you spoke? How did you know? Any non-verbal indications?

Appreciation

- "I felt good when . . ."
- "I like it when . . ."

Life Map

Grades: 3-adult
Time: 30 minutes
Grouping: tribe
Materials: large sheets of paper, colored crayons or markers

What's Your Bag?

Grades: Grade: 3-adult
Time: 1 hour
Grouping: tribe
Materials: paper bags, paste, magazines, scissors, stapler

Objectives

1. To build inclusion
2. To present uniqueness of oneself

Instructions

1. Have people meet in tribes.
2. Give each group one bag per member, a pile of magazines, scissors and paste.
3. Instruct people to makes their bags into a personal collage, using pictures and phrases from magazines. The outside of the bag represents one's public image and interests. The inside contains one's private world or less shared world.
4. Tell everyone that they may staple their bags shut if they want to insure privacy for their inside world.
5. Invite group members to take turns sharing the outside of their bags offering rationale for some choices; each member may or may not share a part of the inside world at time of activity or later date.

Discussion

Ask questions such as:
- Why are people laughing?
- Did people start giving pictures to one another?
- Do you think your bag is a true representation of yourself?
- What did you learn about yourself? About the group?

Reflection

- How did you feel?
- Did members share both parts of their bags? Why?
- How do you feel about group now?

Appreciation

Invite statements of appreciation:
- "I felt good when . . ."
- "I like your bag because . . ."

Slip Game

Grades: 3-adult
Time: depending on group size
Grouping: full or tribe
Materials: question slips; paper bags

Objectives

1. To build inclusion
2. To promote personal sharing
3. To learn subject matter facts or review for a quiz

Instructions

1. Instruct people to sit in a circle.
2. Pass pre-prepared bags (one for each group) containing question slips to each group. Each slip has a question such as, "When are you really happy?", "What is the most special positive quality about you?", "When have you felt very proud?" There should be one slip for each participant, plus a few extra. Ask people to draw the questions with eyes closed.
3. People have the "right to pass" if they do not like the question that they draw and may select alternative ones from those that remain in the bag. They must put the original slip back after taking an alternative one.
4. Have people take turns reading and answering their questions. Remind people of their right to pass. If it is a subject matter question, ask others in the group to give an answer if the person requests assistance.

Discussion

Ask questions such as:
- Does anyone want more information from someone who shared? (If so, then ask; again the person has the right to pass.)
- Would anyone like to respond to a question someone else drew?

Reflection

Ask questions:
- Was it hard to share?
- Did others listen? How did you know?
- Did people feel more comfortable about sharing as the activity progressed?

Appreciation

Invite statements of appreciation:
- "I'm a lot like you when . . ."
- "I admired you for . . ."

SLIP GAME: Sample Questions

What makes you angry?

What makes you happy?

What makes you sad?

What do you do for fun?

Do you have any pets?

What is your favorite food?

What is your favorite place?

What is your favorite animal?

What is your favorite sport?

What is your favorite song?

What is your favorite TV program?

What do you and your friends do for fun?

If you could have one wish, what would it be?

What famous person would you like to be?

What period of time, past or future, would you choose to live in?

What foreign country would you like to visit?

What would you like to be really good at?

What is your favorite story?

What is one food you don't like?

What do you do when you feel lonely?

What would you do with one million dollars?

Would you rather be rich, famous or happy?

What would you do if you were president?

What would you do to improve school?

What qualities do you look for in a friend?

Who is the best person in the world?

What do you do when you get really angry?

Objectives

1. To build inclusion.
2. To give an opportunity to create a visual illustration of oneself from four time perspectives.

Instructions

1. Ask people to meet in tribes.
2. Give each person a "Look at Me" worksheet and colored crayons or markers with which to draw himself/herself as a baby, as a 3-year old, now, and 5 years from now. (Use your own to illustrate.)
3. Ask group members to share his/her four drawings explaining any anecdotes or details that seem appropriate.
4. Remind listeners to give full, undivided, caring attention to the speaker.

Discussion

Ask questions such as:
- What differences/similarities are there between what you are now and 5 years from now?
- Did this activity help you to know group members better?

Reflection

- How did you feel as you drew yourself?
- Was there anything frustrating about this activity?
- At what age do you feel most comfortable? Why?

Appreciation

Invite statements of appreciation:
- "I felt good when . . ."
- "I understand how you felt when . . ."

Look At Me!

Grades: 4-6
Time: 45 minutes
Grouping: tribes
Materials: "Look at Me" worksheet, crayons or markers

Tribes Program Handout

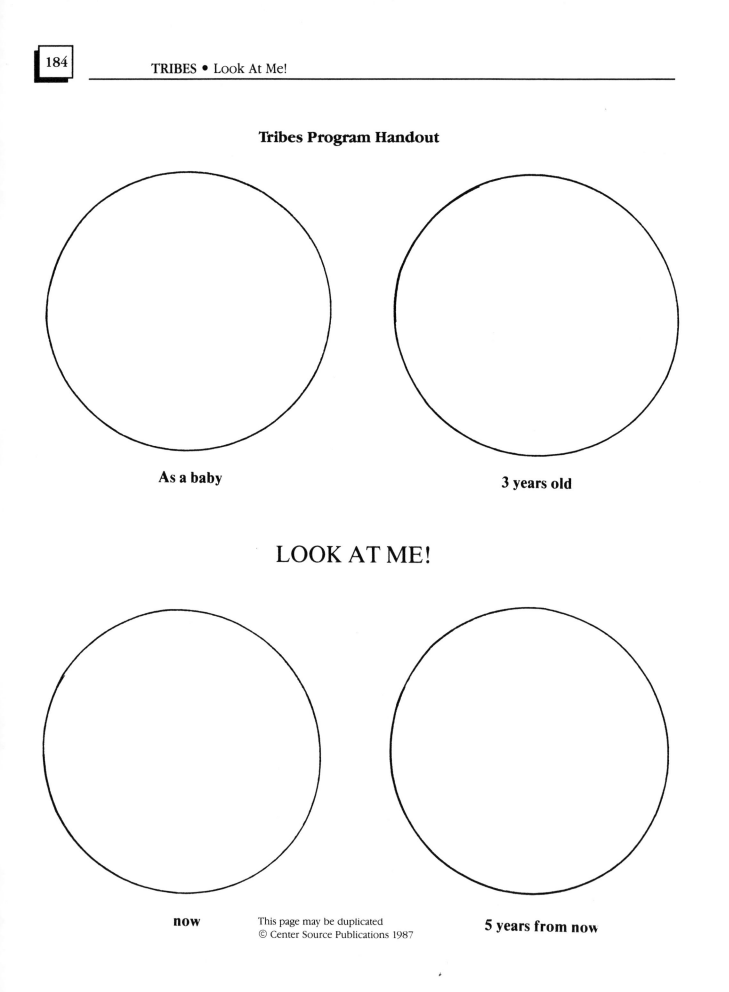

As a baby

3 years old

LOOK AT ME!

now

5 years from now

Objectives

1. To promote personal sharing
2. To build trust in group
3. To problem-solve privately

Instructions

1. Have people sit in full or small groups.
2. Give each person 2 index cards.
3. Ask people to write 1 or 2 secrets about himself on the cards. For example, these could be secret fears, concerns, hopes or feelings that no one knows. Tell people not to write their names on the cards, but when completed to drop the cards in a paper bag in the center of the group.
3. Ask each person to draw one card from the bag. If one's own card is drawn, the person may put it back, or choose to keep and share it as if it were someone else's card. People who choose to pass and did not fill out cards do not draw.
4. After everyone has drawn secret cards, each person in turn around the group reads the secret on his card as if it were his own secret. Suggest that people put themselves in the shoes of the person who wrote the secret, and then elaborate on what that means and how the person feels about it. Think how it would affect one's life to have that secret; it it is a concern or problem, what the person might consider doing. (Take one minute per person to share anonymous secrets.)
5. After all secrets have been shared, group members may comment or give feedback on any secret.

Discussion

Ask questions such as:
- What did you notice that these secrets have in common? What uniqueness?
- How many of you could identify with others' secrets? And what might this mean about you as members of your group?

Reflection

- How hard was it to share these secrets?
- How much harder would it have been if you had told your own secrets?
- Were people listening? How could you tell?
- What differences did you notice in people's comfort or discomfort as the activity progressed?
- Did anyone hear any good suggestions for his or her own concern?

Appreciation

- "I liked it when . . ."
- "I admired you for . . ."

Secrets

Grades: 4-adult
Time: 25 minutes
Grouping: tribe or full group
Materials: index cards, pencils, paper bags

Urgent!

Grades: 4-adult
Time: depending on size of group
Grouping: full group or tribe
Materials: none

Objectives

1. To provide an opportunity to think of a significant other person in one's life
2. To encourage communicating with a special person
3. To promote caring and acceptance for the concerns of others

Instructions

1. Have people seated in a circle.
2. Invite people who care to participate, send a verbal message to a person in his life with whom he feels an urgent need to communicate. Messages can involve suggestions for change in a person's life, a re-affirmation of caring and friendship, and so on. Model a message yourself.
3. The format for a message is: "Dear . . . , I urge you to . . ." Sign the message verbally by saying: "Your . . . (adjective) friend . . . (name)"

Discussion

There is no follow-up discussion after this activity. All messages are sent in an atmosphere of total acceptance.

Appreciation

Invite statements of appreciation:
- "I liked it when . . ."
- "I felt good when . . ."
- "I appreciated it when . . ."

One-Minute Autobiography

Grades: 3-adult
Time: 20 minutes
Grouping: triads or tribes
Materials: none

Objectives

1. To give each person an opportunity to share his/her background
2. To build inclusion

Instructions

1. Have people form triads.
2. Instruct the group that each person has one minute to tell his/her personal biography to the other two members of the triad. The two listeners are to give full attention without interrupting.
3. After one minute, notify people to change roles, giving a different person an opportunity to share. Repeat the sharing until all three people have shared their stories.

Discussion

Ask questions such as:
- When was the last time you experienced 60 seconds of uninterrupted listening?
- Was a minute long enough? Too long?

Reflection

- How did you feel?
- Were the other people listening? How did you know? Any non-verbal indications?
- Did the third person seem to share more of himself than the first?

Appreciation

Invite statements of appreciation:
- "I liked it when you said . . ."
- "I felt good when . . ."
- "I was particularly interested when you . . ."

Tribe Graffiti

Grades: 3-adult
Time: 60 minutes
Grouping: tribes
Materials: butcher paper, crayons or felt pens

Objectives

1. To encourage the sharing of feelings and beliefs
2. To gather and appreciate a wide range of points of view
3. To review subject matter in cooperative learning groups

Instructions

1. Ask people to meet in tribes.
2. Distribute pens and a large piece of paper (at least 2' × 6' long) labeled with one of the following subjects (or an academic topic) on each.

   - Pet Peeves
   - What I Wonder About
   - Ambitions
   - Favorite Moments
   - Things That Scare Me a Lot
   - Things That Excite Me

3. Invite people to write "graffiti" on the paper for 3-5 minutes, all writing at once.
4. At the end of 3-5 minutes ask all to stop writing and then rotate the paper to the next tribe so that each tribe now has a different graffiti paper upon which to write for the next 3-5 minutes. Continue this procedure until all tribes have had a chance to write graffiti on all five large sheets.
5. Return original papers to tribes and allow the members time to read, discuss, and note similarities that occur in the graffiti.
6. Have each tribe report findings back to the whole group.

Discussion

Ask questions such as:
- Which graffiti topic was most meaningful (easiest, hardest . . .) for you?
- Can we generalize about the kinds of things that the group wrote as a whole?

Reflection

- How did group members interact?
- Did what you wrote tell you anything about yourself?

Appreciation

Invite statements of appreciation:
- "It was helpful when you . . ."
- "I liked it when you wrote . . ."

Campaign Manager

Grades: 4-adult
Time: 1 hour
Grouping: tribe
Materials: small circles of paper 3″ diameter, 5″ × 8″ cards, pencils

Objectives

1. To build inclusion
2. To foster positive feelings among total class
3. To build self-esteem

Instructions

1. Ask participants to meet in tribes.
2. Instruct each member of group to write his/her name on a slip of paper and drop it into a bag.
3. Have each participant draw a name out of the bag. Inform each member that he/she is the "campaign manager" for the person whose name has been drawn. The person has been nominated for "Wonderful Person of the Year."
4. Have people interview their candidates if they need more information on special qualities; when ready, each person then designs a campaign button using a circle of paper and lists on the 3″ × 5″ card three good campaign statements promoting the nominee.
5. Have each "campaign manager" deliver his/her campaign speech and present his/her nominee with the campaign button. Lead applause and cheering.

Discussion

Ask questions such as:
- Was it easy or hard to design a campaign?
- Did you notice any similarities among the different campaigns?

Reflection

Ask questions such as:
- How did you feel when your manager was presenting your campaign?

Appreciation

Invite statements of appreciation:
- "I liked it when . . ."
- "I felt good when . . ."

Personal Journal

Grades: 4-adult
Time: on-going
Grouping: tribes
Materials: notebook for each student

Objectives

1. To allow time and privacy for reflecting personal learnings
2. To provide a method for noting personal goals, commitments, hopes and growth
3. To facilitate sharing of personal observations

Instructions

1. Allow regular time for each student to write up personal experiences, reflections, learnings in an on-going folder of tribe activities in which she has participated. Tell people that no one has access to another's Personal Journals without permission.
2. Periodically urge people to review and compare their recent entries with former ones, and to congratulate themselves for signs of growth or learning. Suggest they write "I Learned Statements."
3. People may share things from their Personal Journals with their tribes, if and when they choose to do so.

Discussion

- Do you like keeping a Personal Journal?
- What sorts of information are most of us keeping in our journals?

Reflection

- How does it feel to have a personal data bank?
- Would you like to share any changes you've noticed in yourself?
- What are you learning about yourself through your Journal?

Appreciation

Invite statements of appreciation:
- "I appreciate your need for privacy because . . ."
- "I liked it when you . . ."
- "I think it's neat that you . . ."
- "I value who you are because . . ."

Objectives

1. To build self-esteem
2. To promote inclusion
3. To act out or role play dilemmas or problem situations
4. To structure cooperative learning lessons (history, literature, drug education, social science etc.)

Instructions

1. Ask people to meet in tribes.
2. **Mimes:** Give each tribe a written message or image to act out.
   Example: "the unveiling of a statue."
3. Have each tribe decide how they will portray the message or image without using any dialogue.
4. Instruct each tribe to present their mime to the full group, which then guesses what is being portrayed.
5. **Role-Play:** Once the tribes are comfortable with doing mimes, prepare problem-situations on cards and give to each tribe.
   Example: Brett and Aaron are approached by two friends who ask them to go with them after school to smoke some cigarettes they just found. Act out how Brett and Aaron handle the situation so they feel proud about themselves.

It is meaningful to have the tribes themselves define problem-situations and then exchange them with another tribe to act out. Make certain to follow all presentations with in-depth discussions.

Discussion

Ask questions such as:
* Did the non-verbal actions of the actors in the mime convey clearly what they were portraying?
* Do you ever notice that sometimes people say one thing but their non-verbal actions seem to be saying something different? Can you give some examples?
* What did you think about the way that problem was resolved in the tribe's role play? How would you have handled the situation if you had been there?

Reflection

* How did you feel while you were acting your part?
* Tell yourself one good thing you learned during the role play. (Option: Write about it in your Personal Journal. See previous activity.)

Appreciation

* "I really liked it when . . ."
* "I enjoyed most seeing . . ."

Tribe Mimes and Role Play

Grades: 4-adult
Time: 45 minutes
Grouping: tribes
Materials: none

The Week In Perspective

Grades: 4-adult
Time: 10-15 minutes
Grouping: dyads or triads
Materials: none

Objectives

1. To give each person an opportunity to reflect on recent experiences
2. To increase communication skills and sharing
3. To build inclusion

Instructions

1. Ask participants to form dyads or triads.
2. Tell all that they will take turns interviewing each other on questions that you will give them. Ask them to decide who will be the first person to be interviewed, the second and the third (if using triads).
3. Urge all to give attentive listening to the person being interviewed, and not to discuss anything he/she is saying. Just listen.
4. Example questions:
   "What new and good thing happened to you this past week?"
   "What was hard about your week?"
   "Is there something you meant to do this week but put off?"
   "What one thing did you do that you enjoyed?"

Discussion

- Did you find any of the questions difficult to answer?
- Had you thought back about the last week before today?

Reflection

- What did you learn about you?
- When was the last time you experienced someone caring and listening attentively to your experiences?
- How did you feel?
- How could you tell people were listening well to you?
- How do we feel as a group now?

Appreciation

Invite statements of appreciation:
- "I liked it when you said . . ."
- "I felt good when . . ."

Objectives

1. To create a visual illustration of one's life
2. To encourage attentive listening as an interpersonal skill
3. To promote inclusion

Instructions

1. Have people form triads.
2. Give each person a piece of wire with which to construct a visual illustration of his/her "life to date," the significant trends, patterns and events of his/her years thus far.
3. Invite each person to share his/her "live wire" with other group members, explaining the rationale for its design.
4. Remind people of their right to pass and listeners to give full, undivided, caring attention to the speaker; after the story they may ask questions, express their mutual feelings or concerns.

Discussion

Ask questions such as:
- When was the last time you shared your experiences with others?
- Any similarities among group members' experiences? Differences?
- Did this activity help you to know group members better?

Reflection

- How did you feel as you made your lifeline?
  As you shared with the group?
- Did the group listen while you spoke? How did you know? Any non-verbal indications?
- What did you learn about you? (Suggestion: record reflection in Personal Journal)

Appreciation

Invite statements of appreciation:
- "I felt good when . . ."
- "I like it when . . ."

Live Wire

Grades: 4-adult
Time: 15 minutes
Grouping: triads
Materials: picture wire— 3 feet/person

Client-Consultants

Grades: 3-adult
Time: 30 minutes
Grouping: tribe
Materials: none

Objectives

1. To encourage active listening
2. To experience group support for a concern
3. To assist a peer, colleague or friend to resolve a problem

Instructions

1. Ask participants to meet in tribes
2. Tell people that each will have a turn being a "client." As the client, the person is to share a concern or problem that he/she is experiencing.
3. The consultants (listeners) are to listen without judgment or comment while the client shares problem. They may ask for more information if necessary.
4. Consultants then are to make suggestions to the client for alternatives or solutions to the problem. They are **not** to tell the client what to do, but to suggest many alternatives ("brainstorming" suggestions) concerning the problem.
5. Allow approximately 10 minutes for each client's turn.

Discussion

Ask questions such as:
- How many suggestions did consultants find for your problem?
- Do you have some new ideas that you might try?

Reflection

Ask questions:
- Did the consultants listen well?
- How does it feel to share your own concern with others?
- How do you feel as a group?
- As a consultant, did you feel sympathetic and caring?

Appreciation

Invite statements of appreciation:
- "I felt . . . when you . . ."
- "I cared a lot when you said . . ."
- "I feel I would like to help you . . ."

Cooperation Squares

Grades: 6-adult
Time: 30 minutes
Grouping: tribe
Materials: puzzle sets for each tribe

Objectives

1. To encourage cooperation
2. To help people become aware of their own behaviors which may help or hinder group effort.
3. To build inclusion and influence

Instructions

1. Begin exercise with a full group discussion of the meaning of cooperation. List on chalkboard the requirements for cooperation as generated by full group.
   Example: Everyone has to understand the problem.
   Everyone needs to believe that he can help.
2. Ask people to meet in tribes. Describe the activity as a puzzle that only can be solved through cooperation.
3. Hand out one puzzle set (see next page for instructions) to each tribe.
4. Read or state the following instructions aloud:
   "Each tribe should have an envelope containing pieces for forming five squares of equal size. Each square contains three puzzle pieces. Each tribe needs to select five people and distribute three puzzle pieces to each one of them; the other people in the tribe can be observers. The exercise is complete when each of the five members has formed a perfect square. While doing this, no member may speak; no member may signal for a puzzle piece. Members **can however**, give puzzle parts to others in the tribe if they think they might help them complete their squares.
5. Ask each tribe to distribute puzzle pieces equally among five members.
6. The remaining members are designated "Process Observers" who remain silent during the activity and share their observation after completion of task.

Discussion

- How did you decide who was going to be "process observer" and who was to do task?
- Were you able to work within the rules?
- Did we learn a little about each other?

Reflection

- How did you feel when someone finished his square and then sat back without helping others solve their problem?
- How did you feel when someone held a puzzle piece and did not know you needed it or did not see the solution?

Appreciation

- "I liked it when . . ."
- "I felt good when . . ."

Directions For Making A Set Of Squares

A set consists of five envelopes containing pieces of cardboard which have been cut into different patterns and which, when properly arranged, will form five squares of equal size. One set should be provided for each group of five persons.

To prepare a set, cut out five cardboard squares of equal size, approximately six-by-six inches. Place the squares in a row and mark them as below, penciling the letters a, b, c, etc. lightly, so that they can later be erased.

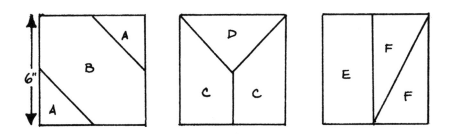

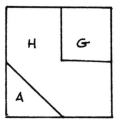

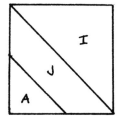

The lines should be so drawn that, when cut out, all pieces marked 'a' will be of exactly the same size, all pieces marked 'c' of the same size, etc. By using multiples of three inches, several combinations will be possible that will enable participants to form one or two squares, but only one combination is possible that will form five squares six-by-six inches.

After drawing the lines on the six-by-six inch squares and labeling them with lower case letters, cut each square as marked into smaller pieces to make the parts of the puzzle.

Mark five envelopes A, B, C, D, and E. Distribute the cardboard pieces in the five envelopes as follows:

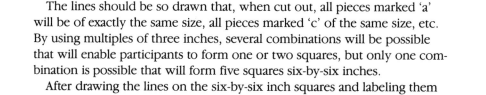

A: pieces i, h, e
B: pieces a, a, a, c
C: pieces a, j
D: pieces d, f
E: pieces g, b, f, c

Erase the penciled letter from each piece and write, instead, the appropriate envelope letter. This will make it easy to return the pieces to the proper envelope for subsequent use when a group has completed the task.

Objectives

1. To encourage active decision making
2. To build appreciation for another's point of view
3. To share a concern or problem anonymously, and have peers give suggested solutions

Dear Abby

Grades: 4-adult
Time: 30-45 minutes
Grouping: tribe
Materials: 5″ × 8″ index cards, small box/tribe

Instructions

1. Have people meet in tribes, and to each group distribute a pile of index cards on which you have previously written a concern or problem (real issues) that children of your class' age level and community might face.
2. Ask group members to each take a turn at reading a problem out loud from a card to rest of the tribe and then say, "If I were Dear Abby I would suggest this person . . . (advice)."
3. Later (same day or a different one) distribute blank cards to tribes and ask each person to write one real concern or problem on an index card to the fictitious news columnist, "Dear Abby."
4. As before have all the cards put in a tribe box, redistribute them back to tribe members to suggest what they, as "Dear Abby" would advise the person to do.

Discussion

Ask questions such as:
   • Did you notice certain types of problems occurring more frequently?
   • What did you think about people's solutions?

Reflection

Ask questions such as:
   • What did you feel when you listened to other people's problems?
   • Is there more than one solution to a problem? How did you feel about your solution?

Appreciation

Invite statements of appreciation:
   • "_____, you were a good listener . . ."
   • "_____, I liked it when you said . . ."

Unfinished Fantasies

Grades: 2-adult
Time: 30 minutes
Grouping: sub-group
Materials: none

Objectives

1. To promote inclusion
2. To develop greater awareness of self
3. To encourage the development of imagination

Instructions

1. Form groups of three.
2. Present an unfinished fantasies and ask the groups to think of endings. Following are some examples or create one of your own.
   - You are eating lunch in a school cafeteria. You get your lunch and walk into the lunchroom. The lunchroom is crowded and noisy with lots of people laughing and shouting and having a good time. Off in a corner is a boy sitting all alone at a table. What do you do? What happens?
   - You are sitting in a class. Several persons in the class are making belittling comments towards another student. The student is obviously having her feelings hurt. She catches your eye and looks at you. What do you do? What happens?
   - You are sitting in a classroom. A student whom you don't know has constantly bugged the teacher and caused trouble ever since the class began several months ago. Although he is often funny, everyone is fed up with his behavior. He comes into the room and takes a seat next to you. What do you do? What happens?
3. Each member of the triad thinks about her or his ending to the fantasy situation and then shares it.
4. Have people decide which endings will be the kindest, most helpful or positive for people.

Discussion

- Do situations like this occur often?
- How do people generally react to this type of person?
- What was this person feeling?
- What did you learn about yourself through this ending to the fantasy?

Reflection

- How do you feel about the way you ended the fantasy?
- Did you identify with the person in the story?
- How do you feel about the others in your triad?

Appreciation

Invite statements of appreciation:
- "I liked it when . . ."
- "I'm like you when . . ."

Objectives

1. To reflect upon personal situations
2. To commit to new attitudes, behaviors or achievements
3. To experience support from peers to encourage change

Instructions

1. Ask each group member to identify a personal behavior, attitude or achievement he/she would like to make.
2. Tell people that by writing a "personal contract," an agreement with oneself, change is made easier. Explain that a contract is a commitment that is specific, believable, and attainable in a certain period of time.
3. Give people time to consider and then write a self-contract as follows:

   "I, (name), will (describe specific commitment or action) by (note specific date).

   Signed: _____

   Witnessed: _____

   Witnessed: _____

4. The author of the contract asks two other group members to sign as witnesses and be supportive of change to be made.
5. Author may ask peers to check on specified date to learn of progress on contract's completion.
6. All the contracts for tribe members may be kept in an envelope for periodic review.

Personal Contract

Grades: 4-adult
Time: 15 minutes
Grouping: tribe
Materials: paper, pencils

Discussion

Ask questions such as:
- Did you have difficulty narrowing your choices to one improvement?
- Do you think that writing a contract for yourself will help you fulfill your commitment?

Reflection

Ask questions such as:
- How did the witnesses feel?
- How does your contract make you feel?

Appreciation

Invite statements of appreciation:
- "I felt good when . . ."
- "I like my contract because . . ."

Space Pioneers

Grades: 4-adult
Time: 35 minutes
Grouping: tribes
Materials: pencils, paper

Objectives

1. To give practice in assessing different qualities and opinions
2. To encourage sharing
3. To encourage understanding and acceptance of others' perspectives
4. To provide an opportunity to look at evolving styles of communication and leader-behavior within the group

Instructions

1. Tell "Space Pioneers" story (on next page) while students are seated in tribes.
2. Write the list of "Advisors" or a similar list of your own selection, on the blackboard for all to see.
3. Ask each participant to identify the five advisors he/she would want to help settle the newly discovered planet.
4. Suggest that each tribe appoint someone to take notes.
5. Announce that each tribe will have fifteen minutes to reach a consensus on which five advisors they would take into space.
6. Ask each group to present its final list to the full group.

Discussion

Ask questions such as:
- What do you see as the main purpose of the Space Pioneers?
- Would you want to go on this trip? Why/why not?

Reflection

- How did your group make its selection of five people? Was it an effective way to come to an agreement?
- How did you feel about your tribe's choice?
- How did people react when you shared your choices? Did they listen? Did they seem to care?

Appreciation

Invite statements of appreciation:
- "I liked it when . . ."
- "I admired you for saying . . ."
- "I'm much like you when . . ."

Related Activities:

- Agree on a name for the new planet.
- Share with your tribe what one personal possession you would take with you.
- Brainstorm and agree on what supplies, equipment, etc. you would need.

Space Pioneers

A new planet has been discovered in our solar system. This planet resembles Earth in every way, except that there are no human beings living there. Our government wants the students of this class to be the first pioneers to settle on the newly discovered planet. They want you to select five adult advisors that you think would be valuable on the new planet. Select from the following list of ten people:

1. Zelda Learner, age 45. Elementary school teacher.
2. Oroville Oates, age 41. Farmer.
3. Clara Kettle, age 34. Cook.
4. Dr. Margarita Flowers. age 27. Botanist.
5. Woody Hammer, age 56. Carpenter.
6. Flo Nightingale, age 37. Registered nurse.
7. Betty Bechtel, age 32. Engineer.
8. Melvin Melody, age 24. Musician.
9. Reverend Adam Goodfellow, age 51. Minister.
10. Roger Kraig, 30. Professional baseball player.

Tower Building

Grades: K-adult
Time: 20-30 minutes
Grouping: tribes
Materials: 8½″ × 11″ paper, tape

Objectives

1. To promote an awareness of influence issues
2. To explore non-verbal communication
3. To build team cohesiveness

Instructions

1. Pass out 15-20 pieces of paper and 1 roll of tape to each tribe.
2. Tell people that they are to **non-verbally** construct a tower or castle using only the given supplies, and that they shall have 10 minutes to complete the task.
3. At the end of the 10 minutes, stop the action.
4. Have all the tribes view each other's buildings.
5. Ask them to return to their tribes for discussion and reflection (which is the important part of this activity).

Discussion

- Did you have enough materials? Would more or less be helpful?
- What does it take for team projects to work well? (How many of you have heard about Japanese management?)

Reflection

- What was happening in your group? Who started the building? Did leaders change? Did any people just give up?
- Were you aware of any feelings among people? Share them with your tribe.
- What was the best thing that happened? What made you feel good? Frustrated? Sad?
- What non-verbal signals were people giving to each other either concerning the tower or their feelings?
- What did you learn about you? Is this your usual style in working with others? Are you an effective team member? How would you like it to be?

Appreciation

- "I appreciated it when . . ."
- "I thought that . . . was very . . ."
- "Our tribe is . . ."

Resentment/ Appreciation

Grades: K-adult
Time: 10 minutes
Grouping: full group
Materials: none

Objectives

1. To teach I-messages
2. To develop oral language skills
3. To learn acceptable ways to express feelings

Instructions

1. Set aside five to ten minutes daily for this activity.
2. Explain terms:
   Resentment: negative feelings concerning something that happened
   Appreciation: positive feelings concerning person or event
3. Review or teach I-Message framework for expressing either negative or positive feelings (see Chapter 4). Post the sentence framework on the blackboard.

   I am (name the feeling) when (name the behavior or event).

   Examples: "I am angry, Tyler, when I cannot have my turn."
   "I appreciate Cary's thoughtfulness in making hot chocolate for all of us."
4. Review the Tribe norms.
5. Ask for volunteers who need to express an appreciation or resentment. It is important to follow-up with a child privately if any statements of resentment are expressions of a serious concern. Follow-up general statements concerning the whole class with the full group. Encourage class to solve problems that may pertain to all using problem-solving techniques suggested in Chapter 5.

Discussion

- Does it help for people to have a way to express feelings?
- Why do you think it is important?

Reflection

- How do you feel now that you were able to say what you felt?
- How was it for other people who listened?

Appreciation

- "I admire you for . . ."
- "I learned . . ."

Use the next activity, **Confrontation**, as a possible follow-up.

Confrontation

Grades: K-adult
Time: 15-40 minutes
Grouping: full group
Materials: none

Objectives

1. To provide a way to work out problems which occur between students
2. To enhance self-awareness
3. To reduce tattling
4. To teach communication skills

Instructions

1. One day when a problem between two people comes to your attention, invite everyone to sit in one large community circle.
2. State the problem or have people involved describe it.
   Example:
   Tanya: "Dawn keeps moving ahead of me when we are supposed to take turns."
   Dawn: "No, I don't, Tanya is always pushing people."
3. Review the norms carefully, and instruct the full group to listen attentively but without comment.
4. Have the two children involved sit facing each other in the center of the circle.
5. Ask each child to tell the other what she is feeling about the problem situation by using I-messages; help them phrase the situation each is upset by if you need to.
6. Ask each to repeat back exactly what the other one stated.
7. Then ask both what each could personally do to help resolve the situation.
8. If they have difficulty, turn to the rest of the class for suggestions. (No judgments who is right or wrong).
9. If the discussion wanders, ask leading questions to re-direct the children to the problem. If the problem cannot be solved set a time to work with the pair privately.

Discussion

Ask questions such as:
- Is it important for people who are upset to tell each other?
- What did you learn as observers?
- Does this issue (whatever was discussed) affect anyone else?

Reflection

Ask questions:
- How do you each feel now?
- What feelings did you have while this was going on?

Appreciation

Invite statements of appreciation:
- "I admire you for . . ."
- "I learned . . ."

Objectives

1. To realize the importance of caring attentive listening in relationships
2. To strengthen listening skills
3. To be aware of non-verbal behavior as part of communication
4. To promote an awareness of the pain experienced when one is excluded from a group

Active Ignoring

Grades: 5-adult
Time: 30 minutes
Grouping: tribes
Materials: none

Instructions

1. Have people seated in tribes.
2. Discuss the importance of inclusion within groups, families, communities and the class. Tell students we will conduct a little experiment to learn how people feel when excluded.
3. Ask for one volunteer from each tribe. Have them step out of the room, waiting for you.
4. Brief tribe members in the room that when their person comes back, all are to go on talking to each other about some subject of their choice; but while talking they are to ignore, turn their positions away from and not listen to the person coming back.
5. While the tribes are choosing their subjects, talk to the people in the hall, saying that they are to go back to their tribes and attempt to tell them something special about themselves.
6. Allow one minute only for the "ignoring" experience and stop the process. First ask reflection questions.
7. If other tribe members want to have the same experience, take more turns.

Reflection

- How did you feel when everyone ignored you and went on talking?
- How did tribe members feel doing it?
- How were people sitting as they ignored you?
- What kind of gestures did they use while talking?
- Did your feelings change by the end of the one minute?
- What were you doing by then?
- Can you each recall times in your life where this has happened to you? Or when you have actively ignored a newcomer?
- Is there someone in your life you try to ignore?

Discussion

- What happens for people who are continually left out?
- Does the same happen for minorities or small nations?

Appreciation

- "I appreciated . . ."
- "I liked it when . . ."

Family Camp Trek

Grades: 2-8
Time: 45 minutes
Grouping: tribes
Materials: Camp Trek worksheets

Objectives

1. To promote critical thinking
2. To learn to assess and make priorities
3. To share special things about oneself
4. To promote the acceptance of individual differences

Instructions

1. Ask people to meet in their tribes and pass out the Family Camp Trek worksheets.
2. Tell them that they are to imagine that each of their families has been invited on a special three month camping trek next summer in Canada. Each person can carry one backpack; all the other supplies (food, medicines, tents, sleeping bags etc. are being provided). There will be three families in each trek group (about 20 people) and you will have an experienced guide. Your assignment is to make a list of things it would be important or satisfying to have in your backpack because you will be away from home for such a long time.
3. Allow people 10 minutes to make their lists. Then have them share their lists with their tribes.
4. Next have them decide which three items would be the most important and to note them with a star.
5. Again share their lists, but this time explain why these items are more important to them than others.

Discussion

- Why do you think it is hard to make priorities?
- Why is it important in life to do so at different times?
- What happens to people when they do not sort out what is most important in their lives?

Reflection

- How did you feel about having to leave some things out?
- Were you thinking of things just for you or others as well?
- Are there times when you feel sorry to give something up?
- Are there times that you are glad you did?
- What did you learn about yourself?

Appreciation

- "I liked it when . . ."
- "Thank you, . . . for . . ."

Tribes Program Handout

1.

2.

3.

4.

5.

6.

7.

8.

9.

10.

Third Party Mediation

Grades: K-adult
Time: depending on situation
Grouping: full or tribe
Materials: none

Objectives

1. To provide a process for conflict resolution that helps both parties arrive at a mutually agreeable solution
2. To model and teach a third party mediator role (one who does not make judgments or take sides)
3. To develop trust and acceptance of individual differences
4. To build inclusion and yet allow influence (a sense of value)

Instructions*

1. Call together the two people who are in conflict and tell them that it is likely a mutually agreeable solution can be worked out. Ask if they would like that to happen? Make it clear that you will not take sides or set yourself up as a judge.
2. Ask each person, one at a time, to describe the conflict; the other is not to interrupt. Encourage each to focus on what is going on now rather than a list of past grievances. Stick to the content. If they try to interrupt each other or are not listening, ask each to summarize the other's position.
3. Ask each in turn to state how the situation makes him/her feel. Reflect back their feelings to draw out a full description. Have each person rephrase other's feelings.
4. Have both persons in turn state what they would like as an outcome to the conflict. As mediator, encourage both to modify their "ideal state" and decide what they would be willing to give up and work toward. Help them look at alternatives.
5. Have both parties acknowledge what changes they each are willing to make in a specific period of time.
6. Draw up a list of the steps each agree to take. Include a time for checking back with the mediator to evaluate how well the solution is being carried out.

Discussion

- Is it helpful for people to have a third party mediate disputes? Why? Can you think of any important applications?
- Were you aware the mediator used specific steps to help the two parties get to a mutual agreement? (List the steps.)

Reflection

- What did you feel as we worked through your conflict?
- Did your feelings change throughout the mediation?
- How do you feel now towards the other person?
- Observers: What were you feeling for the parties?

Appreciation

- "It was helpful when you . . ."
- "I appreciated . . ."

---

*The method can be used with groups as well as individuals.

Thumbs Up, Thumbs Down

Grades: K-adult
Time: 5-10 minutes
Grouping: full group
Materials: none

Objectives

1. To encourage active decision-making
2. To encourage the visible expression of opinions
3. To accept individual differences

Instructions

1. Have all seated in circle.
2. Demonstrate 5 different ways people can vote or express their opinions on an issue. If you . . .
   Strongly agree: wave both hands in air, shout yea, right on, bravo, etc.
   Agree: raise your hand
   Disagree: put your thumb down
   Strongly disagree: thumbs down, stamp feet, boo, hiss, etc.
   No opinion: fold arms across chest
3. Then ask in rapid-fire sequence controversial questions appropriate to age level and interests of the group.
   Examples might be:
   "How do you feel about . . . eating at McDonald's?"
   "Playing soccer? Skateboards? Jumping rope?"
   "People helping each other in tribe learning groups?"

Discussion

Ask questions such as:
- How is this type of voting different from other voting you've done?
- Do you prefer a particular way? Why?
- Did your friends vote the same way you did? Does this matter?
- Let's have some group members toss out some ideas for other issues we can vote on . . .

Reflection

- Were you tempted to change your vote after you looked around you?
- How did you feel about making your values known in public like this?

Appreciation

Invite statements of appreciation:
- "I felt good when . . ."
- "One thing I like about this group is . . ."

Put Yourself on the Line

Grades: 3-adult
Time: 15 minutes
Grouping: full group or tribe
Materials: none

Objectives

1. To practice taking a stand among peers
2. To build appreciation for the different opinions in a group
3. To use as a structure to promote critical thinking on curriculum topics and issues

Instructions

1. Ask everyone to stand up.
2. Describe an imaginary line down center of a room. Identify the two polar positions at either end of the line as "strongly agree" and "strongly disagree." State that the center of the line is for those who have no opinion, choose to pass, are non-risk takers or compulsive moderates. The imaginary line may be called a "continuum."
3. Tell people to move to a place on the line that expresses their feelings or opinion about issues that you will call out to the whole group. For example, "Where do you stand concerning these statements?"
   • It's O.K. to talk to strangers on the street.
   • It's important to always please the teacher.
   • One should never climb dangerous mountains.
   • Always do what your friends do so you won't be left out.
   Have students suggest other topics; use for curriculum.
4. Have people meet in tribes to share feelings on some particularly controversial topic.

Discussion

Ask questions such as:
   • Did you notice where others placed themselves?
   • What did you learn about other members of the group? About yourself?

Reflection

Ask questions such as:
   • How did you feel about publicly taking a stand?
   • Were you tempted to change your position after you looked around you?

Appreciation

Invite statements of appreciation:
   • "I felt good when . . ."
   • "One thing I like about this group is . . ."

Where Do I Stand?

Grades: 3-adult
Time: 15-40 minutes
Grouping: full group or tribe
Materials: animal signs, string, tape

Objectives

1. To encourage sharing
2. To encourage acceptance of individual differences

Instructions

1. On large cards, print four animal names: LION, DEER, FOX, DOVE.
2. Suspend the animal signs from the ceiling in four areas of the classroom.
3. Ask each person to stand under the sign for the animal that he/she is most like when in his/her tribe. Encourage people to talk among themselves while they are deciding where to stand.
4. When everyone has chosen an animal and has taken a place under a sign, ask people to share why they placed themselves where they did.
5. Continue the activity by repeating steps 3 and 4 with other situations:
   • How you are with your friends?
   • How you are with your family?
   • How are you by yourself?
6. Ask people to return to their tribes and talk about their choices and why they stood where they did.
7. A good option or follow-up is to have all write in their Personal Journals their personal learnings from the experience.

Discussion

Ask questions such as:
   • What are the qualities of a lion? A fox? A dove? A deer?
   • What did you learn about other people in the class? About yourself?

Reflection

Ask questions such as:
   • Was it difficult to make choices?
   • Was it scary to share your reasons in the full group?

Appreciation

Invite statements of appreciation:
   • "I know just how you feel when . . ."
   • "I was interested when . . ."
   • "I felt good when you said . . ."

One, Two, Three

Grades: 3-adult
Time: 10-15 minutes
Grouping: sub-group or tribe
Materials: pencils, paper

Objectives

1. To make choices between competing alternatives
2. To allow persons to affirm and explain their choices
3. To practice decision making

Instructions

1. Ask people to meet in tribes or form groups of 4 to 6.
2. State that you will be asking them to make some choices by ranking three alternatives in order of their importance or preference. Tell people to write down the three things you say and then put a number 1, number 2 or number 3 after each item according to which one is chosen 1st, 2nd and 3rd. Examples of questions might be:
   • Where would you rather be on a Saturday afternoon? At the beach? In the woods? Window shopping downtown?
   • Which do you consider most important in a friendship? Honesty? Loyalty? Generosity?
4. Ask tribe members to share their choices with each other and explain why they made the selections.

Discussion

Ask questions such as:
   • Is it difficult to make choices?
   • How did your choices compare with those in your group?

Reflection

   • What feelings did you have when you had difficulty choosing?
   • Does this ever happen in your life about more serious things?
   • What have you learned about yourself?

Appreciation

Invite statements of appreciation:
   • "I liked it when . . ."
   • "I appreciated your dilemma when . . ."

Goal Storming *

Grades: 3-adult
Time: 1 hour
Grouping: full group or tribe
Materials: newsprint paper, markers, tape

Objective

1. To enable a large group to identify shared goals and concerns
2. To structure interest related work groups

Instructions

1. Decide upon a relevant question for the full community to address: (Example: "Where would we like to go on a field trip?")
2. Ask participants to form small groups or meet in tribes.
3. Review rules for "Brainstorming":
   D–defer judgement
   O–off-beat, original
   V–vast number
   E–expand, elaborate
4. Ask each group to choose a recorder and then to brainstorm for five minutes, listing all goals or ideas.
5. Ask the recorders to read all the ideas to the full group.
6. Instruct each group to form a consensus on three ideas.
7. In the full group, record the three ideas from each group on a single sheet of paper or the blackboard.
8. Discuss the ideas as a full community. Combine and/or eliminate ideas that are similar or repetitive.
9. At this point choose among several options:
   • Form task or interest groups around listed concerns
   • Vote as individuals to determine highest priority
   • Compose a "group contract" which includes all concerns for on-going discussion and work.

Discussion

   • Was this a productive session? Why, or why not?
   • Did different groups develop similar priorities?
   • Are the priorities listed a true indication of the group's real concerns or goals?
   • How does this process compare with other goal setting formats?

Reflection

   • Did you feel your group worked well together?
   • Were people listening to each other?
   • How do you feel about the group's priority?

Appreciation

   • "I liked it when you . . ."
   • "I felt good when . . ."

---

*Goal Storming is a variation "Brainstorming." The group should first become familiar with the Brainstorming process. (Refer to: To Build a Better Bathtub, in Inclusion activity section).

Our Treasury

Grades: 3-6
Time: 1 hour
Grouping: tribe
Materials: none

Objectives

1. To allow for individual influence
2. To practice group decision-making

Instructions

1. Ask participants to meet in tribes.
2. Give each group a fictitious sum of money (or paper money) which is to be their tribes' treasury
3. Tell each tribe to brainstorm the best uses of this money. (Review brainstorm process if necessary.)
4. Have each tribe decide what three things they would spend their treasury on out of brainstorming list.
5. Ask each tribe to report their decision to the total group.

Discussion

Ask questions such as:
- Was it easy for your group to come up with ideas?
- Were there many differences of opinion in your group?
- Is it hard for you to decide how best to spend your own money?

Reflection

Ask questions such as:
- How did you feel about the choices your group made?

Appreciation

Invite statements of appreciation:
- "I appreciated it when . . ."
- "I knew what you meant when you said . . ."
- "I liked it when . . ."

Objectives

1. To reach a consensus or agreement on shared concerns, ideas or priorities
2. To build tribe-team cohesiveness

Instructions

1. Pass out 5″ × 7″ cards to each person in tribes.
2. State the decision that the class will try to make together. (Example: field trip sites that would be fun and interesting).
3. Ask each person to write down five ideas to the question.
4. Ask each person to get together with one or two people from his/her tribe, compare lists, and together agree on four ideas, eliminating all others.
5. Ask those pairs and triads within each tribe to meet with other pairs or triads of the tribe and agree on three ideas, eliminating all others.
6. In the full group, ask each tribe to report their three choices. Keep a "running list" on the chalk-board.
7. Once you have a full-class list, eliminate some items through discussion; then use "sticker-voting" giving each person an opportunity to vote for his/her three top choices. (See "Step-By-Step Process For Group Problem-Solving," Chapter 5).

Add up value of stickers to determine the one final choice of the class.

Consensus-Building

Grades: 3-adult
Time: 25-40 minutes
Grouping: tribes
Materials: 5″ × 7″ file cards

Discussion

Ask questions such as:
- What were your reasons for choosing these alternatives?
- Do you see any relationship or similarities among the alternatives we have agreed upon?

Reflection

Ask questions such as:
- Was it difficult to come to agreement with your partners? Why or why not?
- How did you come to agreement? By voting, bargaining, discussing, one person just telling the others?
- To what extent do you feel that you had influence on the group's decision?

Appreciation

Invite statements of appreciation:
- "I like our choices because . . ."
- "I felt good when . . ."
- "Our tribe is neat because . . ."

Peer Response Huddle

Grades: K-adult
Time: 15 minutes
Grouping: tribes
Materials: none or index cards
Subject: any curricula

Objectives

1. To structure a cooperative learning experience
2. To develop energy and interest in curricula
3. To build pride in one's tribe

Instructions

1. Have tribe members count off, or number index cards, one for each person, beginning with the number 1. If using cards, pass them around the tribe so that each person has a number.
2. Tell class that you will call out a question, and each tribe has 30 seconds to huddle and decide upon one answer. Then when you call out a number, that person within each tribe will quickly stand up. You will ask the first person that you notice popping up to give the answer.
3. Keep the questions, huddle time and responses going as rapidly as possible so that the energy takes on a "popcorn" effect.

Discussion

- What did you learn that you didn't know before?
- Is this a good way to learn a lot in a short time? Why?

Reflection

- How did it feel to have other people helping you?
- How do you feel about your tribe?
- Shall we use this method again?

Appreciation

- "I liked it when . . ."
- "I want to thank, . . . for . . ."

Objectives

1. To help slower learners understand or learn subject matter
2. To provide peer support for learning
3. To structure a cooperative learning experience
4. To build inclusion and encourage kindness

Tribal Peer Coaching

Grades: K-adult
Time: depending on material
Grouping: sub-groups within tribes
Materials: depending on curricula
Subject: any curricula

Instructions

1. Ask people within their tribes to share which people are very sure that they understand the concept or material from a curriculum unit.
2. Ask if those people would be willing to be "coaches" for a short time to the other people in the tribe who are not quite as sure.
3. Have people pair off in twos or threes so that coaches are in each grouping with student(s) wanting coaching.
4. Suggest some ways, depending on the curriculum, that the coaches can be helpful. Tell them that their goal is to have their students be able to repeat back or explain to them the information or concept being learned.
5. Tell them how much time will be allowed, and remind people of their attentive listening skills.
6. When time is up, ask those who were students to explain to their whole tribe what they learned from their coaches.

Discussion

Ask questions such as:
  • How many people understand the subject better now?
  • What were some of the important things you learned?

Reflection

  • Was your coach patient in explaining things to you?
  • Did you enjoy the process?
  • How do you feel about yourself now?
  • How do the coaches feel?

Appreciation

  • "I appreciated it when . . ."
  • ". . . , you really helped me when . . ."
  • "Thank you, . . . , I think you are . . ."

Jigsaw*

Grades: K-adult
Time: depending on curricula
Grouping: tribes
Materials: depending on curricula
Subject: any curricula

Objectives

1. To structure team-learning/team-teaching in tribes
2. To build academic self-image of slow learners
3. To develop tribe spirit and pride
4. To help each student feel of value to others

Instructions

1. Select a lesson from a curricula unit that you consider appropriate for the following process.
2. Divide it into six equal parts (or the number of members per tribe) and define study questions. Prepare sufficient materials for that many study groups.
3. Explain the Jigsaw process to your class. Then ask them to meet in their tribes.
4. If you have not already done so, engage them with an activity on the personal feeling level to awaken interest.
5. Give each tribe one set of lesson materials, parts 1-6. Ask each tribe to decide who will be responsible for each part.
6. Ask people responsible for Part 1 to form a jigsaw study group; likewise with parts 2-6.
7. Lead the groups in a brief tribal inclusion activity.
8. Tell the groups what their specific task is and the amount of time that will be allowed. Move from group to group, helping only as needed.
9. When all have finished, ask people to return to their own tribes. If you used lesson dittos, pass out the rest of them to group members so each person has a complete set.
10. Beginning with Part 1, ask students to share the material that they prepared in their Jigsaw group; prepare a format for sharing if you think it will help them.
11. After each segment has been shared, take time for a full-group discussion and in tribes to reflect on the experience.

Discussion

- What did you learn that you didn't know before?
- Is this a good way to learn a lot in a short time? Why?

Reflection

- How did it feel to have other people helping you?
- How do you feel about yourself?
- Was it satisfying to teach others what you had learned?

Appreciation

- "I liked it when . . ."
- "I want to thank . . . , for . . ."

*Acknowledgement is made to Eliott Aronson's work (see Resources)

Objectives

1. To encourage cooperative learning
2. To increase awareness of animal families
3. To structure other subject matter where sorting or categorizing are important (geography, arithmetic, parts of speech, history etc.).

Instructions

1. Lead a full-group discussion about cooperation. Emphasize:
   - Everyone wants all people in the group to do well
   - Each person believes that he/she can help the others
   - Everyone must understand the task.
2. Ask people to meet in tribes. Explain that the activity is to put a puzzle together, but that it can only be solved if everyone helps each other (cooperates).
3. Pass out on Animal Triad set to each tribe.
4. Read the following directions aloud:
   "Each tribe has an envelope containing fifteen triangles with the name (or picture) of an animal on each. There are blue, red and yellow triangles. Your task is complete when each of five tribe members has three triangles in front of him/her, and all three of the animals belong to the same animal family. While you are doing this, you must follow the rules which are:
   - No one may speak
   - No one may signal for a triangle
   - Members may give triangles to others, but they may not reach over and just take any.
5. Ask each tribe to distribute the triangles equally among five tribe members giving each person triangles, one of each color, but not in the same "family" (Fox, Dolphin, Koala).
6. The remaining member(s) are to be "Process Observer," who remain silent during the activity and share their observations after the completion of the task.
7. Each tribe works until the task has been completed.

Discussion

- Were you able to follow the rules?
- Did you learn anything about animal families that you did not know before?

Reflection

- What did you find frustrating about this activity?
- What did you learn about cooperation?

Appreciation

- "I liked it when . . ."
- "I felt good when . . ."

Animal Triads

Grades: 2-5
Time: 20 minutes
Grouping: tribes or subgroups
Materials: Animal Triad Sets
Subject: science

Animal Triads*

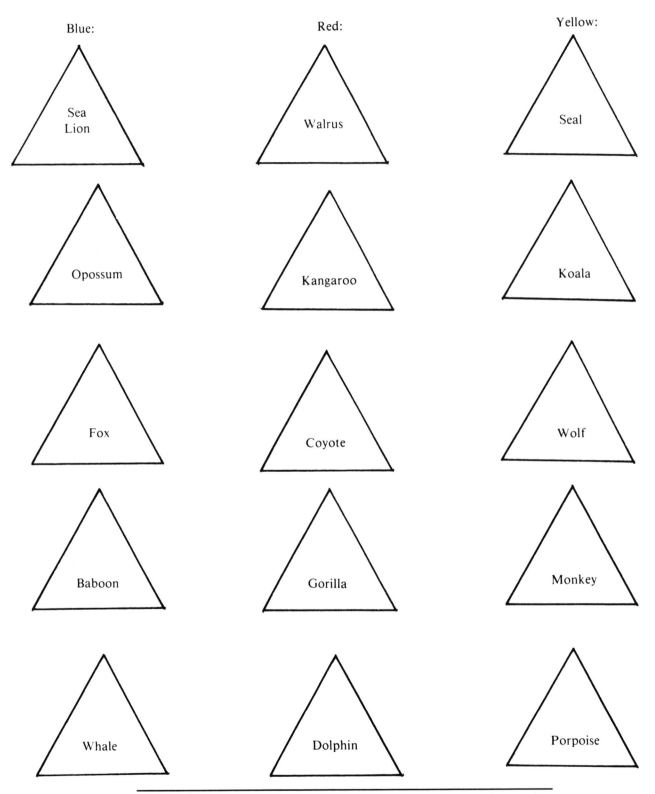

Blue:

Sea Lion

Opossum

Fox

Baboon

Whale

Red:

Walrus

Kangaroo

Coyote

Gorilla

Dolphin

Yellow:

Seal

Koala

Wolf

Monkey

Porpoise

*For use with other subject matter where sorting and/or categorizing are desired, write other topics on color triangles.

This page may be duplicated

® Center Source Publications 1987

Objectives

1. To develop observation and communication skills
2. To practice following directions
3. To understand spatial relationships
4. To learn geometric shapes

Instructions

1. Have children meet in tribes; use aide or cross-age tutor with Kindergarten children if necessary.
2. Have two children in each tribe sit back to back in center of the tribe circle.
3. Tell them that one person will give directions to the other one, and then they will change roles. Have the remaining tribe members sit and observe the two in the center.
5. Give the two partners the same number of the same colored geometric shapes.
6. Tell the "director" to begin moving one of his/her blocks into a pattern, and then describe the placement of the block to the "listener." For example:
   "Put the blue triangle in front of you pointing away from you."
7. The listener is to place the same block in the same position.
8. The director continues adding blocks and describing their positions until a pattern he/she is pleased with is completed (use from 6 to 10 blocks).
9. Have the two partners compare patterns and see how similar or dissimilar they are.
10. After discussion, have other people of the tribe take turns doing the activity.

Discussion

- Were the directions clear?
- What made the task difficult?
- Which shapes were easiest to put in place?

Reflection

- How did it feel to follow directions without seeing the otherperson's pattern at all?
- Did you feel any frustration?
- How do your feel about what you did?

Appreciation

- "It was neat working with you because . . ."
- "You two were a good team because . . ."

Shaping Up With Blocks *

Grades: K-5
Time: 20 minutes
Grouping: tribes, sub-group
Materials: colored blocks
Subject: communication

---

*Method can be used for older students in geography, science and art by giving "director" different materials (maps, patterns, diagrams etc.)

Current Events Debate Circle

Grades: 4-adult
Time: 30 minutes
Grouping: full group
Materials: none
Subject: history, social studies
politics, science

Objectives

1. To enable students to express their views
2. To encourage discussion of current events
3. To enhance people's ability to see different sides to an issue
4. To provide a structure for learning or reviewing curriculum

Instructions

1. Arrange 6 chairs in circle.
2. Tell class that you would like to have 5 volunteers sit in the circle to express their views on (give topic). The extra chair is saved for anyone in the class who wants to come in briefly and add some information to the debate (facts, dates, etc). After adding brief information, person must go back to his/her seat.
3. Instruct the remaining members of the class to be silent until all the people in the circle have been heard.
4. After the circle group has discussed the topic sufficiently, invite other people of the class to direct questions to circle members.

Suggested topics:
- Should skateboards be allowed at school?
- Is it important to go to college?
- Is "Star Wars" a good idea for this country to develop?
- How can people resist peer pressure to use cigarettes, alcohol or drugs?

Discussion

Ask questions such as:
- Did you change your viewpoint after hearing others comment?

Reflection

Ask questions such as:
- Did you feel people were listening attentively to each other?
- How did you feel being inside circle?
- How did you feel being outside circle?

Appreciation

Suggest people make statements of appreciation:
- "I felt good when you said . . ."
- "I liked it when . . ."
- "I am glad you said . . ."

Celebrity Sign In

Grades: 4-8
Time: depending on lesson plan
Grouping: full group, tribes
Materials: 5 empty chairs set in a row front of room
Subject: history

Objectives

1. To structure a cooperative learning experience for history curriculum
2. To enhance communication skills

Instructions

1. Give each tribe the name of an historical character and allow sufficient time for them to learn as much as they can about the person.
2. Set up chairs (number of tribe characters) in a row in front of the room facing the rest of the class.
3. Ask each tribe to select one person who will represent their historical character.
4. As each historical figure takes a chair on the interview panel, have him/her signs in by writing his/her "name" on the chalkboard.
5. Ask each character to tell the other panel members about his or her prominence in history. After all have done so call time out and let tribe members huddle with their character to remind him or her of more data. After several huddles, invite the full audience to ask any questions of the "celebrity" that they still may want to know. Tribe members can also help give the answers.
6. Lead rounds of applause for each character's performance.

Discussion

Ask questions such as:
- Did this activity help you to recall things you had learned?
- How did you choose the historical figure that you portrayed?
- What values were reflected by the characters?

Reflection

Ask questions such as:
- How did you feel portraying your character?
- Did you feel moved by or any alliance to any of the characters as they spoke?

Appreciation

Invite statements of appreciation:
- "_____, I respect you for . . ."
- "_____, I liked the way you portrayed . . ."

Perception And Transmission Of Information*

Grades: 5-adult
Time: 40 minutes
Grouping: full group
Materials: copies of young girl/old woman drawing
Subject: perception

Objectives

1. To promote inclusion
2. To promote an understanding of different points of view
3. To demonstrate how perceptual limitations can affect communications

Instructions

1. Ask people to meet in tribes. Hand out a copy of young girl/old woman drawing to each tribe. Instruct people to glance at picture briefly, without discussion, then collect all copies immediately.
2. Ask people to share what they saw in the picture. Emphasize the concept that people perceive differently by asking questions such as "would you talk to this person on the bus?" or "who in your family does this person remind you of?"
3. Give copies of drawing to each member of tribe and continue discussion.
4. Assist people who have difficulty identifying both aspects of drawing.
5. Expand discussions to other areas in which a person's point of view might be limited by his/her perception of information, (parent/child, teacher/student etc.)

Discussion

- Why did some people see a young girl while others saw an old woman? Is there a "correct" way to see the picture?
- Is anyone able to see both aspects simultaneously?
- How might interpersonal conflicts result from individuals perceiving information differently? How might such conflicts be resolved?

Reflection

- What did you feel towards those who saw the drawing the same way you did? Towards those who saw it differently?
- What did you feel when you "discovered" the other aspect of the picture?

Appreciation

Invite statements of appreciation:
- "I am a lot like you when . . ."
- "I felt good when you said . . ."

*Use prior to history curricula concerning warfare, debates, constitutional rights, different political views etc.; or drug education, viewpoint of parents versus teenager etc.

Tribes Program

Perception and Transmission of Information

© Center Source Publications 1987

Phonic Worms*

Grades: 1-3
Time: 30 minutes
Grouping: tribes
Materials: 6″ circles markers
Subject: reading, phonics

Objectives

1. To build inclusion
2. To strengthen knowledge of letter/sound or sound combinations

Instructions

1. Give each member of the tribes a six inch circle, and give the tribe one extra circle.
2. Discuss and demonstrate the target sound or sound combinations that you want the children to learn.
3. Ask people to write 1-5 words on each circle (depending on the age level of the students); each word is to contain the target sound or sound combination.
4. Have tribe members check each others words to be sure they are correct; if some are not, ask tribe members to help the person find and write an appropriate word.
5. Have the tribe draw a face on the extra circle and paste or staple their "worms" together into a long worm; invite all the tribes to display their phonic worms on the bulletin board.

Discussion

Ask questions such as:
- What did you learn about the sounds? Are words hard to find?
- Did people use a lot of the same words?

Reflection

Ask questions such as:
- How did you feel about other tribe members checking your work?
- How did your tribe decide who would draw the worm's face?

Appreciation

Invite statements of appreciation
- "I liked it when . . ."
- "Our tribe is great because . . ."
- "Thank you . . . I appreciated your help."

---

*The method may also be used well for arithmetic and reading comprehension.

Possessives

Objectives
1. To build inclusion
2. To provide a positive experience using possessives
3. To provide a cooperative learning method for oral and written language, bi-lingual education, and other curricula

Grades: K-3
Time: 30-45 minutes
Grouping: full group or tribes
Materials: paper strips
Subject: language therapy or bilingual education

Instructions

Option A (oral version):
1. Have people stand or sit in a large circle.
2. Beginning with yourself, turn to person to the left and ask a question, such as:
   "What is your favorite color?"
   "What is your favorite holiday?"
   "What is your favorite fruit?"
3. The next student answers, and the first student who asked the question repeats back the answer. Example:
   Student #1: "What's Your Favorite Color?"
   Student #2: "Red"
   Student #1: "Shawn's favorite color is red."
4. Continue the questions around the circle.

Option B (written version):
1. Have tribe members divide up into dyads, and each set of partners decide who is #1 and who is #2.
2. Student #1 asks the question; #2 answers; and #1 then writes the sentence, (Shawn's favorite color is red), on a colored paper strip which has been prepared and given to the tribes.

   " . . .'s favorite . . . is . . ."

3. The partner's then rotate. After all the colored strips are completed, tribes can staple them together and display them.

Discussion
- What similarities did you notice in people's answers?
- Are possessives different after some people's names?

Reflection
- Do you like working together with a partner?
- Did you feel that people really listened carefully?

Appreciation
- "I liked working with you, . . . , because . . ."

---

*The activity can be used for various combinations of curriculum material. A variation on Option A is to have students ask each other across the circle; or integrate it with the Spider Web activity (Inclusion section). For Option B, older students may work in groups of three or four, asking and recording knowledge learned on any subject matter.

What Will Happen Next?

Grades: K-8
Time: 20-30 minutes
Grouping: tribes
Materials: paper, pencils, crayons
Subject: reading comprehension

Objectives

1. To encourage critical thinking skills
2. To build inclusion
3. To structure a cooperative learning experience

Instructions

1. Read (or have students read to each other) a story, stopping in an interesting and/or suspenseful part.
2. Have each tribe write what they think will happen next; they may also want to draw one large picture of their episode.
3. Ask them to present their versions of the story to the entire class. Lead much applause after each one.

Discussion

- How did your tribe decide how to go about writing the story together?
- Did people respect the norms?
- How did our class stories differ from one another?

Reflection

- Did anyone not have their idea used? How did you feel?
- Did you enjoy working together rather than alone?

Appreciation

- "I'd like to thank . . . for listening to me."
- "I felt good when . . ."
- "I was excited when . . ."

Objectives

1. To build inclusion
2. To structure a cooperative learning experience
3. To increase members knowledge of curricula information

What's In A Name?

Grades: 4-8
Time: 45-60 minutes
Grouping: tribes
Materials: butcher paper colored pens
Subject: social studies, history or science

Instructions

1. Have each tribe draw the name of a well-known figure that may be the subject of history, social studies or science curricula.
2. On a large piece of butcher paper, have them write the name vertically with colored pens.
3. Challenge them to research and write a phrase or fact about the person's life after each letter of the name. Example:

W as President from 1789-1797
A lways told the truth, it is said
S uffered at Valley Forge in 1777-1778
H ad 3000 of his men die at Valley Forge
I n no political party as the President
N ever stopped drilling his soldiers in the winter
G oing on for 6 years of war, the British were tired of it
T wo years after Yorktown, British and Americans signed a formal treaty
O n October 19, 1781, was surrendered to by Cornwallis
N ever gave up in the Revolutionary War

Discussion

- How many people knew all those facts before? How many knew about half of them?
- Was it difficult to find the information? Did you check all the facts out?

Reflection

- How did your tribe organize yourselves for the task?
- Was everyone included in doing the work?
- How do you feel about your tribe now?

Appreciation

- "I appreciated . . . 's help and cooperation."
- "I liked it when . . ."

Animal, Vegetable or Mineral?

Part 1

Grades: K-8
Time: 20-30 minutes
Grouping: full group
Materials: 3″ × 5″ index cards, safety pins, markers
Subject: social studies, history, reading or vocabulary

Objectives

1. To introduce a unit's vocabulary words and their meanings
2. To build inclusion

Instructions:

1. Give each student a card with a word printed on it from the social studies, science or language unit. If there are more students than words, use some words twice. If words have been only recently introduced, a word list on the chalkboard may be helpful. (Kindergarten students may do this activity with pictures rather than printed words.)
2. Have students pin their card on the back of another student without that student seeing it.
3. Tell students to circulate around the room and ask questions that can be answered "yes" or "no" until they determine what is written on the card. They can only ask each person one question and then must move along to the next person.

Discussion

Ask questions such as:
- What kinds of questions did people ask?
- Were you familiar with the word before?
- Can we make generalizations about the words chosen?

Reflection

- Was it easy or difficult to find out what or who you were?
- Without naming names, did anyone have a problem receiving wrong information?
- Did you enjoy the activity?

Appreciation

- "I enjoyed it when . . ."
- "I liked it when . . ."
- "I'm similar to . . . because . . ."

Objectives

1. To practice group decision-making skills
2. To structure a cooperative learning experience
3. To build group inclusion

Instructions

1. Using the cards from Part 1, have each student write down what he/she thinks is the significance or importance of the particular word in relation to the unit being studied.
2. Ask tribe members to pass the cards around so that each member also writes on the card what he/she thinks is the importance of the word (or concept).
3. After all members have commented, have the cards read within each tribe.
4. Ask them to prioritize (using voting, stickers or a point system suggested by the teacher or themselves) to decide on one sentence which best represents the significance of the word or concept.
5. Use the same process for each of their cards.
6. Read the cards within the tribes or the full community and display them if appropriate so that other's may review them.

Discussion

Ask questions such as:
- How many people learned a lot they didn't know before?
- What were some of the important things you learned?

Reflection

- Was is easy or difficult to come to a consensus about the best statement?
- How did you go about it?
- Did everyone participate in the choice?

Appreciation

- "I liked it when . . ."
- ". . . really helped us when . . ."
- "Our tribes is . . ."

Animal, Vegetable or Mineral?

Part 2

Grades: Grades:4-8
Time: 60 minutes
Grouping: tribes
Materials: paper and pencils
Subject: social studies, history, reading or vocabulary

ENERGIZERS

In the midst of any time together groups of people will periodically experience lower energy within their environments. Concentration becomes more difficult, boredom and sleepiness can set in and will be counterproductive to accomplishing the task at hand. Students especially become restless. They are likely to withdraw or even do the opposite . . . create a disturbance. The remedy? A quick five minute physical activity to revitalize the group. In the Tribes Program we call these activities "energizers."

There are five objectives achieved through the use of energizers:

1. To revitalize the energy of the classroom or a group;
2. To draw people's attention back to the classroom after a time away (recess, lunch break or some other interruption);
3. To shift gears or energy between group activities that contain different content and need for renewed concentration;
4. To provide a way for people to feel connected again with one another; and
5. To have fun!

The pages that follow contain a collection of some favorite Tribe Program energizers. Some of them are more physical than others, and like other activities in this book it is up to you to select the most appropriate ones for your students. Much depends upon the level of trust, that the class is in at any one time, and the age level of your students.

Acknowledgement is made to the **New Games Book** and the **More New Games** book from which many of the activities have been adapted. (See Resource section.)

Activities for Pairs

1. Human Spring
Facing each other, stand palm to palm distance. Move hands back, keeping them up and open. Keeping feet planted, rock into each other. Stop each other with palms, then spring each other back to standing positions. When you are ready, keep moving back.

2. Stand-Off
Stand facing each other, one arm's length from your partner. Place open hands up and out a little from your shoulders. The object is to make your partner lose footing by pushing or hitting his or her hands only.

3. Stand Up
Sit on the ground back to back with your partner with knees bent and elbows linked. Now stand up together. Try it in 3's and 4's.

4. Trust Walk
Have everyone find a partner. One person of the pair volunteers to be led with his/her eyes closed or blind-folded. The other member of the pair leads the person for 5 minutes taking very good care of the blind partner. After 5 minutes switch roles.

Activities for Small Groups

1. Knots

Stand in a circle shoulder to shoulder. Ask all to reach out and grab two other hands. (You cannot have both hands of one person, and you cannot have the hand of persons on each side of you.) If possible, try not to criss-cross. Now untangle so that all are standing in a round circle again.

2. Trust Circle

Make a circle with your tribe or small group. Have one person stand in the middle with his/her eyes closed and feet planted firmly. Have the rest of the tribe members gently push on the shoulders of the person in the middle, making sure he/she does not fall but keeps moving. The group supports the person as he/she rotates.

3. Wink

Stand in a circle with eyes closed. One person walks around the circle and quietly taps the back of one person who will be the "winker". Everyone opens their eyes and begins to mill around the room. If a person has been winked at, she/he must count to 10 silently and then make a scene to let others know she/he is out of the game. The object is to catch the winker before everyone loses. If a person suspects the winker's identity, she says "I have an accusation!" However, there must be two accusers to stop the game. When someone else becomes suspicious, she/he shouts "I have an accusation!" Then both accusers count to three and point to the player they think is the perpetrator (no discussion is allowed). If they both point to someone who is innocent or to different people, they are automatically out of the game. If, however, they both point to the true winker, the game is over.

Large Groups

1. Hagoo

Divide into two teams and form two lines. Have people stand shoulder to shoulder facing a person on the other team. Stand a yard apart. One person from each team will volunteer to walk past each person in the row of the opposite team. The people on the team try to make the volunteer from the other team smile as he/she walks by. No touching is allowed. If the volunteer cracks up he/she must join the opposite team. If he makes it to the end straight faced, he goes back in the row with her original team.

2. Hug Tag

Play this in the same way people play any game of tag, but when two people are hugging they are safe from getting tagged by the person who is "IT."

3. I Like My Neighbor

Have all members seated on chairs in a circle, with one person standing in the middle as "IT." The person in the middle makes a statement such as "I like my neighbor, especially those who are wearing running shoes" (wearing glasses, are over 12, have a birthday in September . . . etc.). All those people who are wearing running shoes must jump up from their seats and scramble to find a chair; the person in the middle also scrambles for an empty chair. The one person left standing becomes the new "IT."

4. I Love You Honey

Have everyone stand in a large circle. One person in the middle walks up to one person in the circle and says, "I love you, honey." The chosen "victim" is to respond, "I love you too, but I'm not allowed to smile," without smiling. It can be said twice to the same person in the same way. Guess what happens. They smile! Right! The smiler may then trade places with the person in the center or join the person in the center in tempting others to smile. The second option is generally easier on individuals in the group than the first option.

5. The Lap Game

Everyone stands in a long line behind each other and puts their hands on the waist of the person in front of them. On the count of "3" everyone sits down on the lap of the person behind them. This can also be done in a big circle.

6. Rain

Have everyone sit in a circle, facing the center. Ask all to close their eyes, pausing for a moment or two to become quiet while each person gets ready to hear the sound the person on the right will be making. Keep eyes closed as the rainstorm begins with the leader rubbing her palms together, back and forth. The person to the left joins her, and then the person to her left, and so on, around the circle. When the leader hears the drizzle sound being made by the person on the right, she starts snapping her fingers. When the snapping action has been picked up by everyone around the circle, the leader switches to hand clapping, then to thigh slapping and finally to foot stomping. After foot stomping, the leader reverses the order of sounds, introducing thigh slapping, hand clapping, finger snapping and finally to palm rubbing. For the last round, the leader stops rubbing her palms and takes the hand of the person on her left. Each person follows suit around the circle until there is silence once again.

7. Do After Me

Sit in a large circle. One person begins by entering the circle and making a gesture, sound or movement (the more ridiculous, the more fun), and then points to someone else in the circle to succeed him. This person makes the same gesture, sound or movement as the preceding person made, and then adds her own performance. She then chooses the next person, and this person need only repeat the preceding action and add one before choosing someone new. The game is over when everyone has had a chance in the circle.

8. Monkey, Elephant, Palm Tree

Form a large circle with one person standing in the middle as "IT." The person in the center first demonstrates positions for people to take when he/she calls out one of the animals or the palm tree. They are illustrated below:

MONKEY   ELEPHANT   PALM TREE

The person in the center then twirls around and points his/her finger at one of the people in the circle and shouts either: "MONKEY, ELEPHANT or PALM TREE." The person pointed to and the two people on either side of her take the appropriate positions with their bodies. The member of the trio that flubs up becomes the new "IT" and goes into the center of the circle to continue on with the game.

9. Skin the Snake

Have people line up one behind the other. Reach between your legs and with your left hand grab the **right** hand of the person behind you. The person in front of you needs to reach back to grab your right hand with their left hand. Once the chain is formed, you're set to go. The last person in line lies down on his back. The person in front of him backs up, straddling his body and lies down behind him. Continue until the whole group waddles back.

10. People Machine

One person begins the activity by assuming a strange position and making a repetitive movement with a repetitive sound. The next person connects physically in whatever creative way they choose making a different movement and sound. People keep adding themselves to the machine. The results are a huge people machine making much noise.

11. Electricity

Have everyone sit down in one large circle, cross-legged, and knees touching. Hold hands. One person starts a squeeze on one side and the next person quietly passes it on around the circle. Variation: start it off by squeezing both sides. Watch it explode. Variation: send an "ooh" or an "aah" the other way.

12. Bumpety-Bump-Bump

Form a circle standing up with a chosen "IT" in the center. The "IT" walks up to you and stands in front of you and says one of the following:

"**Center**, bumpety-bump-bump"
"**Self**, bumpety-bump-bump"
"**Right**, bumpety-bump-bump"
"**Left**, bumpety-bump-bump"

You must say his/her name, your name, or the person's name to the right or left of you before "IT" completes saying "bumpety-bump-bump"; otherwise you become "IT."

9

RESOURCES

9 Resources

Suggested Reading

Briggs, Dorothy Corkille, *Your Child's Self-Esteem,* Doubleday & Co., Dolphin Books, 1975.

Brown, George Isaac, *Human Teaching for Human Learning,* Viking Press, New York, 1971.

Dreikurs, R., Grunwald, and Pepper, *Maintaining Sanity in the Classroom,* Harper & Row, New York, 1971.

Egan, G. and Cowan, M., *People in Systems: A Model for Development in the Human Service Professions and Education,* Brooks-Cole, Monterey, 1979.

Faber, Adele, and Mazlish, Elaine, *How to Talk So Kids Will Listen and Listen So Kids Will Talk,* Avon Books, New York, 1982

Ginott, Haim, *Between Parent and Child, New Solutions to Old Problems,* MacMillen and Company, New York, 1965.

Ginott, Haim, *A Book for Parents and Teachers,* MacMillen and Company, New York, 1972.

Hawkins, J.D., Catalano, R.F., Jones, G., and Fink, D., Childhood Predictors and the Prevention of Adolescent Substance Abuse, *Etiology of Drug Abuse: Implications for Prevention,* National Institute on Drug Abuse Research Monograph 56, DHHS Publication (ADM) 85-1335, Superintendent of Documents, Washington, D.C. 1985.

Hawkins, J.D., Catalano, R.F., Jones, G., and Fink, D., Delinquency Prevention Through Parent Training: Results and Issues from Work in Progress. Paper presented at the JJDP Executive Session on Delinquency Prevention and the Family. Cambridge, Massachusetts, Harvard, 1985.

Johnson, David W., and Johnson, Roger T., *Learning Together and Alone: Cooperation, Competition and Individualization,* Prentice-Hall, Inc., New Jersey 1975.

Johnson, David W., Maruyama, G., Johnson, Roger T., Nelson, D., and Skon, L., Effects of Cooperative, Competitive and Individualistic Goal Structures on Achievement: A Meta-Analysis, *Psychological Bulletin,* 1981, Vol. 89, No. 1. (pp.47-62) Judge, Jeanne, Student Team Learning, *American Education,* December 1978, (pp. 28-32)

Lyons, Virginia M., (Ed.), *Structuring Cooperative Learning Experiences in the Classroom: The 1980 Handbook.,* Minneapolis, A Cooperation Network Publication, 1980.

Perry, Lee, and Murray, D.M. The Prevention of Adolescent Drug Abuse: Implications from Etiological, Developmental, Behavioral and Environmental Models, *Etiology of Drug Abuse: Implications for Prevention,* National Institute on Drug Abuse Research Monograph 56, DHHS Publication (ADM) 85-1335, Superintendent of Documents, Washington, D.C. 1985.

Poirier, Gerard A., *Students As Partners In Team Learning,* Center of Team Learning, 1738 Capistrano St., Berkeley, California, 94707, 1970.

Redl, Fritz, *When We Deal With Children,* The Free Press/MacMillen & Co., New York, 1966.

Robins, Lee N., and Pryzbeck, Thomas, "Age of onset of drug use as a factor in drug and other disorders", *Etiology of Drug Abuse: Implications for Prevention,* National Institute on Drug Abuse Research Monograph 56, DHHS Publication (ADM) 85-1335, Superintendent of Documents, Washington, D.C. 1985, pp. 178-192

Roy, Patricia A., (Ed.), *Structuring Cooperative Learning Experiences in the Classroom: The 1982 Handbook.,* Minneapolis, A Cooperation Network Publication, 1980.

Slavin, Robert E., Synthesis of Research on Cooperative Learning, *Educational Leadership,* May 1981, Vol. 38, No. 8, (pp. 655-659)

Tanner, Laurel N., *Classroom Discipline for Effective Teaching and Learning,* Holt, Rinehart and Winston, New York. 1978.

Tessler, Diane, *Drugs, Kids and Schools,* Goodyear Books, Scott Forseman and Co., Glenview, Ill., 1980.

White, Earl, *Nourishing Self-Esteem, A Parent Handbook for Nurturing Love,* Whitenwife Publications, 149 Magellan St., Capitola, Ca. 95010 1981.

Wyckoff, J., and Unell, B., *Discipline Without Shouting or Spanking,* Meadowbrook Books, Simon & Schuster, New York

Classroom Materials

California Department of Health, *Friends Can Be Good Medicine: A K-12 Curriculum About Relationships and Well-Being,* California Department of Health Publications Unit, 1600 9th St., Sacramento, Ca. 95814, 1981.

Canfield, Jack, and Wells, Harold, *100 Ways to Enhance Self-Concept in the Classroom,* Prentice-Hall, Englewood Cliffs, New Jersey, 1976.

Carothers, J., and Gasten, R., *Helping Children Like Themselves, Activities for Building Self-Esteem,* R/J Associates, 564 Tyler Ave., Livermore, Ca. 94550, 1978.

Galbraith, R.E., and Jones, T.M., *Moral Reasoning: A Teaching Handbook for Adapting Kohlberg to the Classroom,* Greenhaven Press, New York, 1976.

Gordon, Thomas, *Parent Effectiveness Training,* Plume New American Library, New York, 1975.

Gordon, Thomas, *Teacher Effectiveness Training,* Peter H. Wyden Company, New York, 1975.

Johnson, David W., and Johnson, Roger T., *Learning Together and Alone: Cooperation, Competition and Individualization.* Interaction Book Company, 162 Windsor Lane, New Brighton, Minnesota 55112, 1975.

Johnson, David W., and Johnson, Roger T., *Joining Together: Group Theory and Group Skills,* (2nd Ed), Interaction Book Company, 162 Windsor Lane, New Brighton, Minnesota 55112, 1982.

Johnson, David W., and Johnson, Roger T., *Structuring Cooperative Learning: Lesson Plans for Teachers,* Interaction Book Company, 162 Windsor Lane, New Brighton, Minnesota 55112, 1984.

New Games Book, Ed: Flugelman, A., Double Day/Dolphin & Company, Inc., Garden City, New York, 1976.

Reasoner, Robert W., *Building Self-Esteem,* Consulting Psychologists Inc., Palo Alto, Ca. 1982.

Slavin, Robert E., *Using Student Team Learning,* (Revised Ed.), Center for Social Organization of Schools, The Johns Hopkins University, 3505 N. Charles Street, Baltimore, Maryland 21218, 1980.

Saskatchewan Department of Cooperation and Cooperative Development, *Working Together, Learning Together,* The Stewart Resources Center, S.T.F., Box 1108, Saskatoon, Saskatchewan S7K 3N3. 1983.

Training

Throughout the years of the Tribes program, we have indeed known many people who bought the Tribes book and implemented the process effectively without first experiencing the program in a training session. It certainly can be done, particularly if you have had experience in other interaction process groups.

Tribes is, however, a process most readily learned by teachers through our newly designed "TLC" (Tribes Learning Cooperatively) 30 hour training session. The session prepares teachers to use Tribes as the foundation for other cooperative learning methods. TLC Educational Consultants are available to conduct on-site training throughout the country.

Consultation and training may also be arranged for the use of Tribes with special education students, multicultural populations, year round school programs, and staff management. In addition, a four day Training-of-Trainer (T.O.T.) session will be available by October 1990 for the many districts needing their own TLC trainers to conduct on-going teacher training.

For information, write or phone:
TLC Associates
c/o Center Source Publications
305 Tesconi Circle, Santa Rosa, CA 95401
(707) 577-8233

Notes

1. Bloom, Benjamin S., *Human Characteristics and Human Learning,* McGraw Hill, 1976.

2. Lewin, Kurt. Environmental Forces in Child Behavior and Development. In *A Handbook of Child Psychology,* ed. C. Murchison, Clark University Press, Worcester, Mass. 1931.

3. Bronfenbrenner, Urie, *The Ecology of Human Development, Experiments by Nature and Design,* Harvard University Press, Cambridge, Massachusetts, 1979.

4. Bellah, R., Madsen, R., Sullivan, W., Swidler, A., and Tipton S., *Habits of the Heart, Individualism and Commitment in American Life,* Perennial Library, Harper & Row, New York, 1985.

5. Cooper, S.D. Survey on Studies on Alcoholism. *The International Journal of Studies on Alcohol,* 18 (7), 1983.

6. Robins, L. and Pryzbeck, T., "Age of Onset of Drug Use as a Factor in Drug and Other Disorders," *Etiology of Drug Abuse: Implications for Prevention,* National Institute on Drug Abuse Research Monograph 56, DHHS Publication (ADM) 85-1335, Superintendent of Documents, Washington, D.C. 1985.

7. Egan, G., and Cowan, M. *People in Systems: A Model for Development in the Human Service Professions and Education.* Monterey, CA. Brooks-Cole Publishers, 1979.

8. Carmella Cellini Smith, Marriage Family & Child Counselor, Consultant and Tribes Program Trainer, Center for Human Development.

9. Coopersmith, Stanley, *Antecedents of Self-Esteem,* W.H. Freeman and Company, San Francisco, 1967.

10. Briggs, Dorothy Corkille, *Your Child's Self-Esteem,* Doubleday and Company, Inc., Garden City, N.Y., 1975.

11. Johnson, D.W., & Johnson, R.T. Type of task and student achievement and attitudes in interpersonal cooperation, competition, and individualization. *Journal of Social Psychology,* 1979, 108, 37-48.

12. Glasser, William, *Control Theory in the Classroom,* Harper & Row, New York, 1985.

13. *Magic Circle,* Bessell, H. and Palomares, U., Human Development Program, La Mesa, California.

14. *Schools Without Failure,* Glasser, W., Harper & Row, New York, 1969.

15. We acknowledge these concepts to Thomas Gordon, *Teacher Effectiveness Training,* New York: Wyden Co., 1975.

16. *The Warm Fuzzy Story,* Steiner, Claude. JALMAR Press, Inc., Sacramento, CA., 1977. Dr. Steiner has given permission for the use of an abbreviated version of this story contained in Chapter VIII of this book.

17. The term, I-Message, was first developed by Thomas Gordon, *Teacher Effectiveness Training,* New York: Wyden Company, 1975.

18. Raths, Harmin and Simon, *Values and Teaching,* Merrill Company Publishing, New York, 1966.

19. Johnson, David W., and Johnson, Roger T., Cooperative, Competitive, and Individualistic Learning, *Journal of Research and Development in Education,* Vol. 12, No. 1, 1978.

20. Lott, Albert J. and Lott, Bernice W. "Group Cohesiveness and Individual Learning." *Journal of Educational Psychology,* 57: pp. 61-73, April 1966.

21. Fox, R., Luszki, Margaret B. and Schmuck, Richard. "Social Relations in the Classroom," Diagnosing Learning Environments, Chicago: SRA, Inc., 1966.

22. Acknowledgement is made to Elliot Aronson, Ph.D., for his pioneering work and evaluations of this process. *The Jigsaw Classroom,* Sage Publications, Beverly Hills, California, 1978.

ACTIVITIES INDEX

Code:

Inclusion activities are noted "INC"
Influence activities are noted "INF"
Subject matter activities are noted "SM"
Energizers are noted "EN"

Activity, Code and Page Number

INDEX

About the Author

Jeanne Gibbs is the founder and former Executive Director of the Center for Human Development, a California (non-profit) Corporation, dedicated to the prevention of behavioral problems and the promotion of well-being for children and their families. Originally she was a chemist from Northwestern University, who became more interested in the chemistry of people and the systems in which they live. Working in the field of drug abuse prevention for more than fifteen years, she has been committed to researching, designing and pioneering environmental approaches to human development. As a consultant she works nationwide with a wide range of schools, youth serving programs, community organizations and human service agencies.